MURMUR
LAURA MULLEN

FUTUREPOEM BOOKS
NEW YORK CITY
2007

MURMUR
"'APPROXIMATION DEMONTABLE'"
LAURA MULLEN

FIRST EDITION | FIRST PRINTING

This edition first published in paperback by Futurepoem books
www.futurepoem.com
Editor: Dan Machlin
Guest Editors: Ammiel Alcalay, Jen Hofer, Prageeta Sharma

Design: Anthony Monahan (am@anthonymonahan.com)

Cover image © Bridget Walsh Regan (bridget@bridgetregan.com)
Interior flap image © Anthony Monahan

Typesetting: Garrett Kalleberg
Copyediting: Marcella Durand

Opening quote from Wilkie Collins, *The Law and the Lady*, Chapter XIV. New York: Penguin Books, 1998.
Quote, p. 67, from Gertrude Stein, "Forensics," *How to Write*. Los Angeles: Sun & Moon Press, 1995.
Quote, p. 125, from Gertrude Stein, "Marry Nettie," *Writings 1903–1932 Volume 1*. New York: Library of America, 1998.
Quote, p. 132, from Alain Robbe-Grillet, *Le rendez-vous*. New York: CBS College Publishing, 1981.

Cover and text set in Scala, Berthold Akzidenz-Grotesk and Chalet.
Printed in the United States of America on acid-free paper.

This project is supported by an award from the National Endowment for the Arts, and by grants from the New York State Council on the Arts, the New York Community Trust, and the Fund for Poetry. Futurepoem receives nonprofit sponsorship for grants and donations through Fractured Atlas Productions, Inc., a 501(c)3 tax exempt organization. Contributions are fully tax-deductible and much needed!

Distributed to the trade by Small Press Distribution, Berkeley, California
Toll-free number (U.S. only): 800.869.7553
Bay area/International: 510.524.1668
orders@spdbooks.org
www.spdbooks.org

"I drew down the blind and lit the candles. In the quiet night—alone and unaided—I took my first step on the toilsome and terrible journey that lay before me. From the title page to the end, without stopping to rest and without missing a word, I read the Trial of my husband for the murder of his wife."

—Wilkie Collins

for my mothers

THE AUDIENCE

The roll of double-strength paper towels is printed with images of trees, she notices, tearing them apart as she uses sheet after sheet in the effort to swab up the mess. With any luck, she's thinking, bitterly, we'll be getting burgers in Styrofoam packages stamped with palm fronds and the rapidly vanishing species of the rain forest. There's always a March to attend or a Special to watch and buttons and T-shirts and bumper stickers to buy, she's thinking: the first response to any donation is inevitably a request that one repeat it, at once. Has life ever seemed this worthless, and one's own skin so worth saving at the same time? The gestures are empty, the characters chant at the dinner table, the gestures have to be made. The wife of the famous dead writer is remembering him at some sentimental length; he's known for what he didn't say: he lent a pressurized-by-its-reticence tragic glamour to a measured combination of spiritual impotence and physical violence. The thus and such review arrived today, full of the usual stories about upper-middle-class white people (in which the deepest emotional experience available to the characters is dismay), and lower-class types, the preference being for Southerners, who feel everything, intensely. (Southerners being allowed feeling as women and certain specific ethnicities are—in exchange.) If something does, despite everyone's best efforts, actually happen in these stories, the characters react with—depending on their class, race, gender, sexual orientation, and background—voluble but meaningless shock, sorrow, and possibly horror, or silent but *meaningful* dismay. There are no stories at all about the war or shopping, and few about politicians or the extremely rich. You don't see executives, swaying slightly in the jostle and press of the subway rush hours, reading fat dog-eared paperbacks slipped into homemade or store-bought book covers, bits of pretty ribbon to mark the stop. In the books for which the advances are listed in the Business section, she moans and feels herself go soft and wet, he feels himself getting hard, silently, and the places they are going, the things they are wearing and eating and driving around in and buying for each other function as an elaborately twice-removed system of signs for dimly remembered ideas about style, beauty, and culture, via the use of brand names. There's one dead body, at least. Have personal relationships (so-called "intersubjectivity") become more difficult, or does it just feel that way? Has the work of the host gotten harder, are the guests simply less well-behaved, or has the whole charade just become too impossible, now that we have to perform it successfully while acknowledging, all around, that it is merely a highly self-conscious charade? *What is it to be human now tell me.* Tell me. The pictured trees dissolve in her hands; the rising water's flecked with white. In the apartment above, a husband and wife can be overheard arguing: *"You never . . . , I always . . . "*—their sharp tones and muffled voices, at dawn, a part of the harsh gray light and the unceasing rumble from the street. Of course there's a baby, which sobs and wails and shrieks. So much, sometimes there's a vague uncertain fear—carefully kept vague, kept uncertain—they might be hurting it. Apart from the winter morning their radiator leaked through the living room ceiling, there's been no contact. But they exist up there, like a story written over and over for which there is still an audience, like a story, like a fate.

TABLE

ILLUSTRATIONS

Memory Marriage Murder Mother Mystery Muse Marker Men Mere Mis
placed Memory Market Mulled Monument Mendacity Misprint Mr. Mrs. Mesh
es Machine Milk Marble Menstruation Mercenary Mound Model Mutter Mercu
ry Monsoon Mistral Mond Mess Masterpieces Master Masturbate Movement Mo
ments Mention Marry Murmur Mort Masticate Mop Make Malice Meaning Muse
um Millions Mental Monster Matter Moldovite Mirror May Me Malaprop Meno
pause More Manager Mare Martian Merde Muddle Mad Much Morale Map Mis
ery Marvel Mat Middle Miscarriage Miss(ing) Mulch Mountain Mentor Melt Medi
ate Meditate Medicate Magnetic Motivation Miserable Motif Music Material Mer
chandise Momentum Mind Medley Mouse Misspelled More Murk Modernism Mem
ory Meaning Marriage Meant Mother Murmured Mysterious Muse Me Merely Mis
placed Memorialized Mouth Market Mulled Monument Mendacious Misprint Mo
ments Mention Missing Medicine Momentary Mistake Modus Mediate Muffle Muf
fle Mute Me Memory Marriage Murder Mother Mystery Muse Marker Men Mere Mis
placed Market Mulled Monument Mendacity Misprint Mr. Mrs. Ms. Memory Mar
riage Murder Mother Mystery Muse Marker Men Mere Misplaced Market Mulled Mon
ument Mendacity Misprint Mr. Mrs. Meshes Machine Milk Marble Menstrua
tion Mercenary Mound Model Mutter Mercury Monsoon Mistral Mond Mess Mas
terpieces Master Masturbate Movement Moments Mention Marry Murmur Mor
tify Masticate Mop Make Malice Meaning Museum Millions Mental Monster Mas
tectomy Moldovite Mirror May Me Malaprop Menopause More Manager Mare Mar
tian Merde Min Muddle Mad Much Morale Map Misery Marvel Mat Middle Miscar
riage Miss(ing) Mulch Mountain Mentor Melt Mediate Meditate Medicate Mag
netic Motivation Miserable Music Material Merchandise Momentum Mind Med
ley Mouse Misspelled More Murk Modernism Memory Meaning Marriage Meant Mur
der Mother Murmured Mysterious Men Merely Misplaced Memorialized Mouth Mar
ket Mulled Monument Mendacious Misprint Ms. Meshes Machined Milk Mar
bleized Mound Model Mutter Mercurial Mistral Mess Masterpieces Mourn Mas
ter Movements Masturbate Moments Mentioned Married Masticate Mop Make Ma

Crying out for her ("inconsolable") and then beginning to notice how, heavy with mucus, the pooled saliva in our mouths would, lifted, form (on the repeated "M") a sort of bubble capable of extension, that is to say, which we could blow (very gently), as we exaggerated the trembling sound it contained, this thin film (linking our parted lips) communicating its tensile vibration so we could feel and concentrate on the breath pressing against it: the goal, to try—with care—to animate and not break, to swell at will and shrink and again . . . — starting over with Mmmm . . . . *So that soon, without exactly forgetting our grief . . . .*

A NOUN'S MEANT

(Of course there are two of them since they function as the sides of a gate)

Falls back from the open book the interrupted reader turning inward (where it will)
In her place at first perhaps this inward turning I am a passage then or hollow place
Halted in her reading hand outstretched as if to stay or silence   *would finish*

Open on her lap   the forgotten book

The messenger lifting meanwhile
His admonitory or encouraging hand

                                        enters left

Allegory inevitable? "I'm here now aren't I?"
In her room close closet coffer box this book
     Outside   intelligence arrives in passing passes through her pierces
     singles her out vessel   fingered

                         When did you lose your will exactly
                         What were your desires exactly

Or crosses both hands over her heart   answers a servant
Seemingly gazes inward won't meet his eye can't doesn't not meeting his eye
     is   *seen*

Starts at his entrance (drops her book shields her eyes)   Windblown
Heavy center waiting   for what will through   press   attending
White bird leaking a trickle of gold sand down into the chill dark   in between

Here
Holds in the book she shut a hand pale as the page: she holds her place.
As place(mark)   blank   displaced   her sudden guest
     "I can't quite   place you"
Her other   hand to her heart the messenger still for her response

She looks away gathers around her closer cloak   nothing takes the words back
Touching the lines of text as if she read   blindly   feeling
Head tilted illustration I listen and   "a servant"   she closes the book her hand in it

Enters   *Fail tarry lull efface*

Light in the folds her robe as she turns from her reading half turns the light from the
page on her face a figure for what might the words bleed what she reads coming true

suddenly a white bird hovers its wings pages a cry like a burst of light a stopping place looking up to answer what was not in fact a question although the one who brought word awaits a response   open window between them   reception   dead gaze of he who looks inside to recall exactly in their author's order words not his elsewhere eyes having by heart spoken through her single finger held in the open book as though when left again alone she might return to that page paragraph sentence word "Where was I exactly?" Rereading until abruptly that uneasy sense of recognition stops

                      deep and the tide the currents
                      smoky underwater light

Draws back in the instant of giving in   no / yes   listen   a messenger arrives
tilt this gleaming sky   of gold leaf   there are two of them a gate
and between   shape

A message arriving   alights   urges seeks to persuade convince
what will come to pass will come to pass   attend

She lifts one hand as if to ask for silence   as if to say but halt here wait a moment
let me read a little longer   before   holds one hand up the fingers curved yes as
if to say yes of course but oh not yet not please yet

Attend   an instant

Swirling depths of heavy roses warm folds of the red cloth of her dress   disclose

The space that opens between them necessary   space of communication
infinite   elsewhere the speaker whose word within her
the messenger sent to say that already within her   between a space opens past sense
              optimal distance from which

Attend this mouthpiece turned by her strayed gaze to ghost
Unroll from the scroll words held at her high her narrow window
Open between them her good book

From the candle blown out on his entrance a waxy smoke floats slowly up undulates the theme a thin excuse for this glow and sheen of light on the curved edge for instance of a brass candlestick gleaming above a gold head bent

"You'll ruin your eyes reading in the dark like that!"
Mostly entering from the left I enter left my eyes in fact

Interrupt announce   and now for an(other)   word *from*
I walk in she looks up   she's reading   I walk in in the middle
of a sentence   "He came nearer,"
"Suddenly she was aware of his nearness,"   for instance

A caller   what is this place   empty   a room that gives   on a garden
she hears him out
        sets down her book for the sweet-voiced stranger seeking to engage
her   services   oh some white bird dropped pendulum-like sways above them
at the end of a glittering cable above the body contrail of gold leaf in the wake
of the said thing (meant

Here's what will happen he says but he kneels before her to say it
and she   her answer   always
but it happens as he says no matter what

Attend acceptance (speech)
The partition of space (this)

The messenger says nothing stops lifts a white hand flower-like white blooms in
the other motions toward what appears above invisible completes a thought not his
explains the doubled nature of what and she halts in her reading turns abrupt into
terror doubt agreement stopped hands raised in surrender rose in the swirl of hot
orange-red cloth already seems pregnant (oh there's a cat behind her back arched
caught in the act of dashing off

Parted dark   a woman immersed   interposed   an entry wanting
a word with

Enter a messenger bearing   a stem of lilies or unfurling left a scroll his own
mouth shut always   the reader in her coffin-like room   a garden opens
away from   boxed in   with her good book   starts   start here
amaze us   preface

(Start here eye holes in an old wooden door admit through the broken wall your long
your private view her shaved sex wound-like set slightly askew bare limbs akimbo

among weeds aglow in the light she lifts   for instance)

Enclosure   encased

Something someone comes to her at   would speak with   to
she can neither
refuse nor continue   distrusting
eyes fixed on a text she'd have
by heart

An "ugly" death

His look of exhilarated compassion as he can finally explain it now
we who from this distance only want the guilty excised world restored around
an understood   absence

Attend

Flutters shut the all-but-forgotten book white wings close around a white hand hold
still pages where was I body of a bird her hand makes among the feather-like to shut
she after cracks seeking the exact what sounded out the sense of when as if turning
from the future unfolded before her would continue where left off

Bed in the background   reference

Her gestures impossible to interpret securely look sometimes like submission and
sometimes like a weak attempt to hold for a moment meaning back   as music
                                        lull efface

Scent of smoke   entering   a 'fixed' look   'something about his eyes'
they say   who live to   entrance tearing her attention from reluctant
this   leaves   one   finger inserted in the shut she'll come back to to
keep her   place   unrepresented return to the book   which
sentence   reread until the sense of familiarity   stops

"His hands," for instance

In a sea-like blue-green sky from a wound which opens ruffled clouds or waves scar
rippled at its edges finest gold wire light straight into the ear of indentured one who

reading seeks to perfect her already exquisite understanding of a story in which a woman reading is by grace

(Someone noticed at night she sometimes doesn't close her curtains completely, someone has already tried once the basement door and found she isn't always so careful about locking it keeping it locked)

Elect

Holds her hand to her heart as if to still or swear to its startled caught her lashless eyes lowered under the glare white bird in its burst cage above bright spiky halo fracture pattern   radiant

Of course they are set like the posts of a gate   I can't get through   gestures

She lay down. She went to bed early but it wasn't just that. She "took to [her]
Lay on her bed reading murder mysteries, mostly, contemporary gothics, romances
Books stacked on the floor in piles a foot or so deep; arranged on the night table, precariously; splayed beside her open on the bed, like
Skulls on the dust jackets, smoking guns, syringes: a drop of green poison oozed from a needle's tip, pearls, cracked glass, shadows and bloody fingerprints, women fleeing in moonlight—one lit window a sliver of light
She they I looked over our shoulders, running away, or her my our sprawled body the enticement: lying at a strange angle to show off the line of exposed throat and open thighs, eyes shut. Hurried toward or away from
Long hair waving up where the author's name was number of weeks on the list of bestsellers. They just lay there, or rushed to arrive or depart—our erratic footsteps
She drew her knees up, adjusted the pillows, chewed the edge of her thumb or she was smoking a cigarette or winding a lock of hair between her fingers or filing her nails. For awhile she tried worry beads—a short rosary of flat beads of red glass—you could hear them falling against each other, *click click*
She looked up, frowning, anxious: *What*
Wandering patternless
Married for the third time; had two children: they
She looked up: not meeting the "melting" gaze of the man who might save her (potent but not demanding, wildly handsome, charming, and of course
Said yes or no, in answer; her mouth tight, her glance
A smoking gun, a bloodstained knife on the cover of the book brought back up: a vial of pills tipped out; a broken brick wall; a naked body sprawled at the edge of a

landscape
Masked her face
Shut the door again as she requested, left her alone, let her go on reading, promised
Walking out into the suburban streets named for trees and women, we were also
the products of a failed imagination, small cogs in the creaking mechanism of a
dull, obvious

"It isn't so hard," he whispers. "You can do it. Begin anywhere," he says, "make a
mess of it—it's not supposed to be so

Where the "I" has its address as surrender. Mother: where the "I" has its address as
digression a willingness to be no longer the whole story but. Parenthesis. Hand to
the heart as if to calm or claim in the instant of giving place to or becoming a place
from which. Our object of awe and pity interrupted in our reading. What do the
words mean? When she insists she wanted children of what exactly is she thinking?
Is she thinking? I wanted children. What does she mean; what does she think she
means? Having been one of them the word has a particular resonance: it wasn't
possible to desire the experience she seemed to be having (with / through me).

The stage she is   opened   illustration   textbook dissection
from another time   in which the pictured fetus inside her appears
hands to face   ashamed or   reading

"I" already suspect empty place from which to speak or be this speaking for to at
not mine inhabited briefly by me a (m)other place I take in order to speak to locate
my speaking responsible in taking title announcing a site of responsibility podium
impediment necessary over which I leaning louder breathe. Enabling reference
where leased so to speak, "I," I say and she is beside me pointing my hand to my
heart as if trying to still or locate that scared beating. What was it you wanted to say
to me a moment of confusion we seize her see her me in this instant before or at the
exact moment of acquiring perfect belief. "I" and what's meant is at once understood
although of course it means something else entirely   you
     speaking to me

"wanted" desire claimed retroactively an unsteady "I" emptied continual wanting her
to realize a particular which could be answered name here how do you know what you
anyway casting into a future the shifting past uncertain   why weren't we they
"children" beautiful perfect adoring and everyone would if not exactly fall to their

knees at least stop saying you couldn't do anything right at least not any longer say you'd failed at everything

"children" interval true story found the large canvas laid on the floor to dry and onto the surface deliciously slippery leapt skidding across the painting smearing of course before caught out of intelligibility the artwork went into the trash and the children into the bath to be scrubbed you said with a stiff brush and household cleansers detergents

"children" what does the word exactly   a relation   not a thing

A blue cloak pulled across her red dress falling open over the belly we can't help but see as already swollen one hand holding the cloak closed at her throat the other in an open book   a kind of study her communion in there alone with the words   how it all turns out   how it ends   the ending

(Leaves her what's left on that red mattress a rented room painted with her blood disemboweled dismembered her own hand stuck back into the abdomen he emptied as though looking for something)

Entry a messenger raising two fingers   accounts for the duality

Hand held out as to shadow on the empty wall between them (between them in the distance the door to the garden)   (behind her the bed) but there are no shadows here no light source save that delayed arriving rupture   a sky of gold leaf   lilies in one hand   the other   held out
"Don't be afraid"

No identifiable source of light but our looking

Spirit straight secured as she is to the sky
On that single gilded cord or in at least one
Instance of almost defacement a blurred trace
Of failed erasure dragged through the image
Transgressed divides into two equal triangles
Something invisibly passing only the strong
Horizontals verticals architecture holding
The composition together across the literally
Shattering effect of that direct   communication

Not to describe affirm or comment on but will in the instant of its saying come into being

She says yes nods or has nodded or perhaps she has not in fact agreed despite which

(Windows drenched in a roseate light) ("to tell the truth")

The appearance of the messenger   the medium itself   witnesses   "and then"

Figure in a long hallway filling with dusk as if a kind of smoke as if the building were on fire lifts a trembling hand to a door as if to knock runs instead one uncertain finger over the name engraved again all in black as if already

Where she sets her book aside for that   voice   break caress
Seeking to persuade convince

They disappear into the light   in a sky of gold leaf they are made of gold leaf
      image drowning in light

Blazed across   as though to cross out   as though to erase
(They disappear into the light)

She is surrounded by open books pages I cannot cross   the brightness illegible I
      cannot cross   burns between us

A bird in flight or flight itself

Shifting balance of interior and exterior space
She reads or pretends to be reading
(To be alone you can claim to be reading)
You are reading
          broken into
What we see her seeing   what she sees

In what might otherwise be taken for a declaration   shining a division
representing breath guides another arc

We leave her under the eyes of

She turns from her book gaze elsewhere even yet she might be alone might turn
that "inward" look for so we understand it on herself to find another truth rises
        attend   surprised by the messenger's extreme stillness kneeling arms
crossed head bent   completely given over to the words he must   hears him
out who entering left   states

Her body a passage
Intact

Above them that dark sky pierced by a single gold line   her burning head   a
white   bird   incinerated in flight   smoke-thickened air other   finger of
filtered light   of course there are two of them   destined   thin   wind
turning pages

How it ends   how the ending   just like that

BEGINNING AGAIN & AGAIN

Out of the drifting layers of dark chiffon, a black-gloved hand lifts, tentative, toward the handle of a door in the long, dimly lit corridor, and then, relaxing its sketch of a grip, slowly withdraws. Wait

Sand, wind-sifted across a still body. Wave sigh and *hush hush*. Time, as they say, passes. A gray day: sky and ocean matte, and what is it that glistens, obscenely bloated, wet skin stretched taut, supposed to be beautiful still? "I never touched her!" Maybe that's enough. Surf of sheets around the exposed body, below a carefully expressionless face, waiting—afraid to be seen as waiting—for his touch. If. And what uncertainty, just now, makes him draw his extended hand back? Another chance to take a stab at guessing what she might have felt like. "It," he says impatiently, lighting another cigarette, "not 'her,' 'it.'" The victim's just *the washing up*, the body's the relic of a mood that's passed. Ever anything other than this unbearable revelation of *lack*? "Gorgeous." Was the knife a kind of bookmark? And does the story stop there, stop where we set it down, tear the pages out, stop where we stop in our reading, the rest of it vanishing almost without

I'll start with a brief epilogue

Here come the policemen slowly over the beach, wavering like a hallucination, picking their way through the sand spilling into their black shining shoes, holding their arms out for balance; here they come. Here they are, badges aglint in low sunlight, shreds of the warrant fluttering in their raised fists; here they come shouting a warning the wind rips apart, Halt

"The first look could disappoint you, as water near the shore is often murky, or turbid, as

Heavy heat, the damp print left by a clenched fist on the surface of the desk; sunlight like melted butter; drone of a trapped insect. A faint shudder in the pane of pebbled glass in the shut door. A silent telephone, covered in dust. *A sense of time—days, weeks—as weight, crushing into some kind of layer of fossil fuel all the bodies we'd run up against, a black thick liquid of useless guilt and grief . . . .* An ashtray full of butts among which one pale beige filter marked by a smear of hot orange lipstick. Gummy shot glasses randomly stacked; coagulating muck in the bottom of coffee cups; old files splayed open, ash on the papers and photographs, dust sifting down in gold light the tilted blinds slice. *Dressed as if for a funeral, she slowly raises one gloved hand to the veil over her face; murmurs something like*

Somehow to get in the absolute stillness and

The photographers cap their lenses and set down their cameras, the medical examiner shuts his black murder bag; the Jr. Inspector closes his notebook, the Inspector puts out his cigarette—and then they all (the experts gathered around the body) begin loosening ties, bending down to tug at their shoelaces, shrugging off raincoats and the jackets underneath. It's like a locker room suddenly, out there in the middle of that lonely expanse of beach, there's all this awkward camaraderie, horseplay, joshing around: "Hey, it's cold!" "What'cha lookin' at faggot?" "Silk boxers with hearts no less! Check it out!" Until they're naked, goose-pimpled by the seawind, standing around the corpse in a shy circle . . . and then? *What now? What*

I cannot bring myself to keep remembering these incidents over and over again. These are ugly images totally alien to me. I seem to have not participated in them, merely stood by and watched as

"Once you've got something on ice we can discuss it. Until then," the Chief Inspector shakes his head, "it ain't nothing but," smiling to take the sting off, "feminine intuition: suppositions and anxieties, paranoia, a network of nightmare premonitions, nervous guesses taken out of context . . . —seriously, we can't devote any more time to it. No body, no case."

But isn't the complete absence of evidence simply the first precaution a really smart

Try to want something, he pleads, moving away from the bed, more than reassurance, more than just

I removed the plot. I wanted to hear what they were saying. It is not a Silent World at all, but—we are so distant—we come to think of it like that. I lifted away everything necessary for an identification, the rest decayed into the unsteady landscape, and indeed the wild animals did, as he'd promised, help erase what was left. "The entire world is nothing but a memoranda . . . . " I let go of character, working with some uneasy combination of roles, gestures, discourses. I faked the broken arm. Tried pretending I was a cop. Pulled out of context I waited to see how long they would try to maintain the fiction: we were just turning down the lonely dirt road because I'd remembered I'd forgotten . . . something. *This will just take a couple of minutes.* I thought the failure of the definitions would be more obvious: I was always surprised by their trust. Traces a jagged trajectory through an unstable setting, not intact, not

Seen in the half-light of the corridor: her veiled eyes fixed on nothing, wide mouth set in a carefully held half-smile, rouged lips a dark contrast to her livid cheeks. Her gestures seem somewhat mechanical: they have a look, at least, of having been built back into 'gesture' after having been analyzed as movement, seen, say, in a series of still photos, "this is what it looks like . . . . " (So *this* is what . . . .) A widow's dress. Paused a long moment at the shut door, leaning close to the print on the glass: she leans so close the words dissolve into isolated letters . . . —she slides one black gloved hand over the script as if to brush away the language in the way of her effort to understand what

18

Battering the headlands incessantly, waves have carved the rocks into craggy palisades that extend for miles along the coast. In sheltered areas, the shoreline is indented by tranquil bays and lagoons that are enclosed by shifting dunes and grassy lowlands. Special attractions include

What happened to the previous

At her core, the pathologist suggests, there was such an absence, really, so complete an—there's no other word for it—emptiness; it seems strange to make such a fuss about her death. Now we can say she is gone, but I ask you: did she really ever exist? Not, of course, that I'm accusing anyone here exactly of making her up (what an impoverished imagination that implies, morbid if not actually . . .); I'm merely insisting, as someone has to, that she had in fact no essential wholeness, so that to object so strongly to her dismemberment . . . . A shrug. I'm not saying that whoever did this did us any favors, mind you, It's just that she *was*, as the poet says, "a broken bundle of mirrors": crashing into even smaller shards and more dangerous splinters at the slightest

Here they come, as always too late, wavering in this light, mincing through sand that pours like gold gritty water into their gleaming shoes, holding their arms out for balance as they pick their way across the steep sides of the dunes. Here they come at last, badges glowing in the last of the sunlight, bits of warrant fluttering in their raised fists (they all wanted to carry it), each of them shouting "Stop police" as though they gave themselves the order and failed to hear or heed it—look out. Here they come, and we had better, by the time they get here, have some better version of the story straight or at least

There's a woman lying naked on the blood-stained sand, in her abdomen the exact wound so vividly described as given to her ex-husband, metaphorically of course, by her request for money—specifically, for child support. "She's sticking a knife in my gut," he said, backing up and holding clenched fists to his stomach, "and twisting it." Down the beach a silver handbag gapes, spills a scatter of slick pictures out: a cubist rendition of this same landscape. Other evidence: a green lace bra, tangled in trash and drying kelp; a strand of pearls looped through foam scum tracing a departed wave's shape; salt-stained silver satin pumps set side by side on the dune's slope. About two hundred dollars a month. Now the body, closeup: you can see how one hand still moves, smoothing the dark sand, erasing the footprints, already vague enough you'd

Where the head had been there was nothing but

The bed full of sand, invisible, shifting, abrasive, despite the time spent each night tearing the whole thing apart and shaking out—again—the sheets. Sand on the floor, the crunch of it audible crossing the room; in his teeth always the same salty

She sways in the doorway clutching her ripped robe to her chest, one eye already swelling and her lip split. She insists she's fine and he insists she's fine and anyway no one wants

"I called you the hyacinth girl . . . ," the Inspector murmurs, as they turn away from each other, *chilled*, as they'll say, *to the bone*; suddenly shy, picking back up the

Pages erased

The trail cold, the trail "like ice." "Old wounds," the phrase, and, "I know, but." What did you see? What do you recall of what you . . . ; what did someone suggest the truth was once. How stories mutate over time: "That's not how it . . . !" "That's just . . . . " "Not the way *I* . . . . " In the morgue the frigid proof, clumsy stitches wandering her halved

End of the day, end of the season: a faded ocher light in the dry dune grasses, on pale beige sand violet in the hollows. The ocean's a grape-stained blue-purple toward the horizon, blue-green by the shore, an abrupt line between the two shades. A sandpiper nervously stalks its double in the shimmer. Scraps of garish bright color: torn Styrofoam, crumpled plastic bottles, crushed cans, wadded bits of various wrappers . . . . The dull green metal drums, set out at intervals, overflow: gulls perch on piled garbage, screaming and pecking at each other. Teetering on a rim, one steadies itself, opening white wings, sinks its head under the surface layer, comes out with something heavy, and flaps off. On the damp sand at the edge of the water there might be a silk gown—stitched with pearls and sequins—the surf intermittently swells and sucks flat again, filling, emptying out

"'What do you want?' 'What do you think you want?' 'What did you feel you were supposed to want?' All these questions!" She was laughing, but

Underwater light of a windowless bar: on the grimy wood of the counter he pours a small pile of salt, pushes an errant line of white across the rough inscriptions, the hacked out, suddenly brilliant letters, hearts, dates and

Pages damaged
Pages lost

CHEWED *VAGUE*

Okay, spill. But this time, I said, try to start a little closer to something like the beginning. She got up and shut the window. She said *Like you haven't been sleeping much.* Okay, he said, let's hear it again, this time straight. His eyes a little blanker than usual. He put the prologue before the exposition. I thought of what it would mean, that kind of money. If it's a story that's going to take awhile, let's have a drink. Surf booming in the distance. The language of the heroes surprises us so much with its precision and clarity, we at once think we see into the innermost recesses of the bank vault. But you wouldn't believe me at first. My throat felt thick. I said "I don't trust anybody." I'm trying to get at the truth. Of course the words must be understood before anything else, he said, making a production out of getting us drinks. But these are not my words. I rubbed talc on my face to erase the colour, charcoal under my eyes to accentuate a hollow dark look, and dabbed a pale blue on my lips. The phone rings, but there's nobody there: an echoing silence. We prettied it up some before the law got it. I was practically spending the cash. He asked me what it was worth. A long silence. Arrested for speeding, the body in pieces in the back seat. In fact I noticed the case was empty yesterday. Don't try making a song about it. See what I mean? You're getting me all mixed up with someone else. The demand that the woods be understood, "before anything else." Her eyes were icy cold and empty. There was only a counterfeit music—a long irregular line where the water creamed on a hidden sandbar. I'd say we were getting a little closer to the truth. It's a lot of money. He recited again the 'six points of interest.' *I seem to have sent you a letter meant for someone else.* There's another imaginary person in the room who finds my body in the woods. He died before he had a chance to say much of anything. Usually that knife is kept right by the door in this display case. Talk sense. We gathered in the library. "It's me, isn't it." He's just a light picture cast on a dark wall, but he'll talk to you. I blew smoke at the ceiling. What was it he'd said? A paperweight, a letter opener, an extension cord. "Her . . . —oh it's horrible!— . . . . " Another aspect of the *False Self* syndrome. I thought about the money. They got a blurred impression off the glass. The gag in his mouth was warm and wet. I didn't say a word. You knew exactly what was going to happen after that. Only we couldn't figure out how to make the truth stick. On incredibly tiny scales space-time becomes jagged and discontinuous: at those scales space dissolves into a sort of polymer network, like your shirt. When I came around again it was night. You can make miniature waves yourself by blowing across water in a shallow pan. Myth died out there with the genius of music. Figure it out for yourself. The line gave an extra click. I went over to the communicating door and tried it. No footprints, no weapon, no signs of violence—very neat. "This *is* business." The sea at last.

Blue-veined flabby thighs parted worn gray panties broken elastic torn off mimicked What a mess *various objects tried in the yet tight he half knelt on trembling sideways open the words she'd said to him over and not what he saw tearing ragged tendons veins passage the dull blade pulling her skin to part other hand in her thin hair on the blood-slick floor still seeming to go eyes clouded no with each jerking motion hacking at to get entirely off*

He observed that during these first scenes the spectator was so peculiarly anxious to make out the problem of the previous history, that the poetic beauties and pathos of the exposition were as long gone as the features on a body left in the woods for a couple of months. I poured us all another drink. *I had become a living fantasy on a theme in dark and endless . . .,* her voice trailed off. A glimpse underwater will reveal so much you can't really absorb it. He said he had room in his ears. The objects held a message for one and only one of us. The delusion of being able to put a clean bandage on the "eternal wound of existence." Her eyes burned. I let the smoke down into my lungs. "It's better sometimes," he warned me, "not to crack wise." Offshore, distinct zones are difficult to notice. He held the bill up to the light. If the clue leads directly to the suspect there is no room left for the mysterious depths, dark and full of long lace-like things. We watched each other. He repeated, "I'm a busy man." They each took a limb. *You look tired.* The gun pressed against the back of my skull. It's all done with mirrors. Always, at this point, I like to invite the reader to solve it for him—or her—self. There's a chance she was framed. He said she had stars in her eyes. We looked down at the knife-shaped impression in the velvet. I woke up groggy, but dimly recalled someone insisting we should now ask: "In what form does music *appear* in the mirror of motive and deception?" *Now, here is your box with one door, two windows, and solid walls.* We can't do anything without a body. Darkness closed in. Wired for the double zero and snared by the seductive veil. It appears as will: he knew better than to keep insisting he didn't remember. His breathing made a wet sound. I thought of it as *trying to stop something terrible from happening:* I sat in my cell and asked myself what I would say to whoever committed this hideous crime. It is, he said slowly, a lot of money. Whatever rises to the surface in the dialogue appears simple, transparent, and beautiful, but I won't play the sap for you. The room was a ghost from some long-buried memory system. *Blood tells.* I slid a hand into his pocket, but someone had been there before me. Now everything was exactly as it had been on the night of the tragedy. We spent years trying to find out how the bodies were got rid of.

Aperture enough reaching in larynx cut rinsed fine spatter of blood on cracked porcelain shred of flesh smaller than thought squeezed resistant between his palm and the rust spot where the faucet she'd said to tighten remember shut morsel he scoots with the tips of his

fingers into the disposal's gape

Two doors in a blank wall faced with marble, a bullet hole right over the heart, an airtight alibi, which in itself is suspicious. But surely, she laughed, you don't believe that one of us . . . . He insisted on seeing for himself. The door was locked, the window too small to admit anyone. I pulled off the highway and doused the lights, going over the whispered directions the dead man had given us. "Business," he said and cleared his throat. She discovered the body. He stuck to his story. We stayed in the shadows. I thought about it, but what interferes most with the hearer's pleasurable satisfaction in such scenes is an opening in the texture of the previous network. *It's that sort of hole.* Okay, sing! The long-distance or *icicle crime*, as he called it, writing to her. Somebody finds my body. Motive is everything. Then I went along another corridor exactly like the first except that it didn't lead to a long silence. She went by as though she had never seen me before. The way back into the past lay through the mind, but not my mind. The sender's address said simply *From Hell*. Whoever it was went away again. Why that song and dance about the stiff? It's dark in there. I've got a piece that'll buy me some peace, an art that deals only with death. *If there's anyone here interested in doing a little business* . . . . There was a ragged gap in the texture of the story. Of course it's the same weapon! The thickness of the blood, he said, as it congealed, that almost oily feeling. This is so truly the case, that whoever gives himself up entirely seems to see all the possible events take place in himself, yet if he reflects, he can find no likeness between the arrangement and the scenes that passed before his mind. One of the hands of the dead woman had been pushed into her stomach. I was going to turn myself in anyway. Let's go get him while his memory's fresh.

A little water turned off gurgle quiet into which after drip splat splat starting round black
hole in cracked stained white terror or grief look long enough anything's a face O slowly one
dripping hand to the switch hit it on and then as swiftly off "Don't"

Rope, a lot of rope tied in hard knots. That kind of difficulty, he said, wasn't good
for business. Placed in the mouth of a person who could be trusted, the thin places
in the narrative showed up clearly enough. *If the door opens I shoot.* "Destitute of all
hope, he sought the truth," or "Confused, we look for what has vanished." I looked.
"I hoped these uncontrollable events would not affect our relationship." She tore
her dress off. In a thin, desperate voice she went on talking to my back. As dead as
tragedy, his phrase. I'd say we were getting a little closer. A long irregular line where
the water creamed on a hidden sandbar, and a signature below that. In the same way
Descartes appealed to the truthfulness of God. It sounded even worse when I said
it. The shot seemed to come from somewhere about here. I had a feeling she wasn't
giving me the whole story. Nearly impenetrable thickets interlaced by a maze of
placid streams and rivers, they give way to a sprinkling of hundreds of low islands.
"I may send you the bloody knif . . . if you only wate a whil longer."

Hit the switch again let run turned it off a breathy whir before the blades stop "vvvvvvvvv"
voice box stood there looking down might action off feel to find what's left bring up or fingers
down there no and turn the motor on again oh no knuckles edge of livid sink don't boys vox

The language is strained to the utmost that it may *imitate music*: little forms, like
separate sparks, a network. *"Aurelia?"* I said. "To hell with that." *There's a dead body
on the floor and it's still pretty early in the morning.* Self defense can be stretched into

something like a necklace of silvery lights. She was going to be gone, long gone, and I was going to be out of the picture. But an innocent person, he insisted, doesn't become a suspect: a suspect, by definition, isn't innocent. A clean print on the missing half of the mirror. He made me tell him all about it and repeat it verbatim, and then he said I should forget it—in case anyone asked. The exam room was an aquarium, or vice versa. I couldn't imagine her life. These are but a few of the associations along the shore. *You ought to get some sleep.* It's a perfectly natural side of someone to want to survive and avoid the ending when it looks as though only one person could have done this. We all drank and looked very solemn. I wiped off everything I had touched.

My mother is an appliance

To say simply that we desire to hear and that there is at the same time a longing beyond that deep blue. The night was full of sirens. You might want to try lying on a rock and putting your face into the water. Let's talk about the money. I took the safety off. There was more to the story. *This year people are taking the miracle claims made for seaweed's restorative powers seriously.* I append the following plan of the library. It looks continuous but is actually made of one-dimensional threads. He said tragedy was able to deliver us from "the intense longing for this existence." Sometimes I wonder what happened to the rest of it.

DEMONSTRATING BODIES

Opening the chest wall and blowing air through the lungs, for instance, cooling and ventilating the fire in the heart. Thank you. Your witness. *What do you remember; what do you think you remember?* Hunting the passage, a variety of sincerities to choose from, looking for work in show business. Cross examination: having immobilized the ribs, for instance. He wanted to know how they looked on the inside, how they worked. What did someone *suggest* the truth was? They got to talking about what it might feel like to kill someone. You'd be amazed at how much a severed head weighs, for instance. How the story gets told: fragile beginnings, checked, tender and aggressive. Silences. Halts. An entry noting the purchase of one round trip and one one-way ticket. "That's not how it happened!" Tentative rebeginnings, slight discrepancies. Hypothetically speaking, of course. Openings. In the third person with no memory of the bite marks. Oh? How would *you* tell it? The question of who speaks first, and then . . . . "Well, that's how *I* remember it." *Okay, let's hear your version then, honey,* smiling indulgently at everyone else. Or a cryptic inscription and the date when the "fiancée" in question breathed her last. She's fine; we're fine: it won't happen again. Wavering outlines imagined or remembered, sunk in the "waste and empty" sea: sand-blurred, coral-complicated. Asked her if she could help him with his books; showed up in the middle of the night; sat on the floor, naked, crying, "But I thought you wanted . . . . " *I thought you were gonna let me tell it. Honey?* If you could hold a mirror down that open mouth. *Go ahead then, but* . . . . She washes up in pieces at the shoreline, "cargo": traces of a lost, lost . . . . Fell, she said, by accident, an accident. Letters inscribed in a heart in the sand a sudden wave softens. *Like I wasn't there too* . . . . Hauled into my office with the help of the morgue attendants, who booked her, who know the book by heart: "In fact, all you really have to do . . . is show up, relax, pretend you're an actress making a cameo appearance in a movie.

Reread #1: *Be a 'Creature Unlike Any Other'*." Seventy-six feet of tape to hold her in place, slack flesh wrapped in a green sheet, clumsy black stitches wandering her halved face: a speaking likeness. *The dirty platter after the feast.* Underneath their report her voiceless speech, to describe a residual, uncertain . . . —for instance. How would *you* escape? *I'm a woman, I can change my mind. Honestly, honey, you don't seem to trust yourself.* Tears slide from under the lids they've sewn shut. The corpse is despairing, furious. "Cessation of pain," he intones, when she finally stops trying to tell them how she saw it, "is an impoverished wish." I love you. The chair's a loss: stained cushions removed by the attendants and finally burnt. Otherwise nothing has been touched. He glances at the clock, pours himself a drink, insists she also "lied," turning away to reshelve the book, "in every breath." As long as the air was artificially replenished by means of a pump . . . —for instance. He thought of changing his name to that of his last victim; she practiced writing her name as it would look if, if only, if

As this episode begins, our detective's trying to close the massive, over-stuffed binder in which he's collected what he likes to call the "flotsam and jetsam": all he has to show so far by way of a report. Newspaper cuttings, scraps of notepaper, cocktail napkins, cancelled checks, photographs, siftings of tobacco and lint, baggies oozing mysterious fluids, and other (even less mentionable) articles keep falling out. He whistles soundlessly. *Sheesh.* If *he* can't make sense of it, what will anyone else . . . ?! Except to see it, just as it is, as a confession (*I can't figure it out*). Victimless? Motiveless. Maybe not even a crime but a series of unrelated accidents. Not even a series. A few suggestive incidents, between which emerges—it's hard to talk about this—something like an association, a "correspondence . . . . " He's down on his knees, looking for something that fell under the desk. *Oh, boy.* He's a cipher to himself, a blank he musters, we might say, this army of evidence against. Not to say there isn't a murderer, and an empty place in the air that monster will fit exactly into when encountered: a silhouette, extended hands tensed to measure what

Exhibit 1 is admitted to evidence and marked Exhibit 1, 209109-G, October 21, 19 . . .

Light off the blade of the lifted knife

To begin with: a body on the beach. And then the gathered witnesses and experts, contaminating or obliterating by their presence traces of the crime we call the truth: the body less real with every picture they take, every case study, each list of statistics, new proof of their competence. That shocking first pure instant of pity and horror replaced by the increasing conviction that there is always going to be less of whatever it was we thought we came here for, we said we wanted or couldn't admit we wanted: might have killed or actually did kill to get hold of even for a moment. There's a body on a beach on the cover of the book in the hands of a woman who lifts it up, masking her face. We saw the splayed body, gleaming, slick, *I can admit now I was excited.* From behind the spine of *The Body on the Beach* ("Ten weeks on the bestseller list!"), she said this routine was, and here she set the book down on the sand open at her place, deadly, that she was, excuse me, going swimming, even if no one else

End of the day, end of the season: gold light on dull ocher grasses flattened and glittering in the force of the wind, pale beige sand faintly violet in shadowed ridges striping the sides of the low dunes. The ocean calm, fringed at intervals by a vacillating band of white; the water blue-purple out far, a saturated blue-green closer—an abrupt, traceable line between the two colors. A flock of sandpipers skittering uneasily through the surf. On the beach bright bits of litter: broken Styrofoam cups, crumpled plastic bottles, torn aluminum cans and shreds of boxes and bags, all that language: names and claims and ingredients, splashes of garish color. Dull green metal garbage cans are set out at intervals: a gull's perched on the rim of one, wings open, body swaying, it opens its beak as if to cry out, pokes its head down, and rises (something illegible dangling from its beak) to flap off, followed by a crowd of other gulls, screaming. Arrayed above the slowly unfolding fan of surf:

1.   One clutch purse of water-stained quilted green silk stitched with seed pearls, fastened by a small gold starfish; contents: one wine-dark lipstick and a damp wad of cash.

2.   One pair teal satin pumps: heels of transparent Lucite in which faux pearls "float."

3.   One pair violet fish-net pantyhose.

4.   One sequined silk floor-length sleeveless dress.

But no dark shape interrupts the even shine of fading light on the jade-colored crests of the waves, or the smooth cobalt swells farther out.

5.   One giant clamshell.

6. Your head full of myth.

7. It looks like

She reaches into or describes herself, a kind of autobiography, illustrative, "realistic." She stands facing us, naked, holding open the rent flesh: the clearly depicted organs and reproductive apparatus neatly arranged as in a display case. She doesn't look at what she shows us and the dismay on her face—a controlled sorrow faintly tinged with disgust—as she looks away, off, might be for something or someone else. Or we might say it was an inward look. It might be someone or something else she opens for us, so quotidian seems this task of parting the skin and drawing it neatly aside as one might part the velvet curtain of a theater if her ribs, say, were the proscenium arch. She waits there, relaxed, holding apart the clean edges of the cut as far as possible and no blood impedes the gaze meant to penetrate though there might be a stain on the floor she stands on (impossible to be sure in the reproduction): it could be a shadow or the paper might be slightly foxed. In this revision of an earlier image, the deep wound, the site of instruction, is reproduced as an architectural detail on the wall behind her. There the image of the uterus contains a tiny pale fetus that covers its eyes or tries, unsuccessfully, to hide its

"He could've done it any time in a fog like this."

"He could've done it standing practically right next to you: you would never have noticed."

"It could be happening again, right now, anywhere down the length of this long blank beach."

They shiver a little—*Are you trying to scare me?*—look over their shoulders, and laugh

Q. First filed and then polished.

A. There is no other one in existence

Our hero falls asleep at his desk, dreams the interrogation again: the bare room, stained concrete walls, harsh light, one cop yelling *Spill!* While the other, smoother voice whispers, Why make it harder on yourself; We can straighten this out—with your help. *What do you remember?* "Well," he says authoritatively, "a guy like this, I'd guess . . . ." He dozes off over the report he's reading again for the gaps, the lack of connections between events, wakes with a photograph of the body *in situ* stuck to his face. He can still hear those voices: Sure, that's all it is, a mistake; we just need more details, *a name, a number* . . . . —If you can only convince us . . . . He keeps coming back to his own statement: *I glanced over at the thing on the bed. I was trying to remember what had happened but I had a head like an uncleaned fish tank and no idea how long I'd been out* . . . . They can't expect him to sign it. The problem is, he says in the dream, it's all language. He rubs at his eyes. It just seems so distant. He thinks the report should have included physical evidence: a handkerchief glued into the file, say, a piece of rope taped to a description of the rope—there's really no substitute. *I had a feeling there was something here I was supposed to be able to think about, but the question of identity came first.* The teeth they'd removed should be in there, right next to the dental records, and the amputated hands ought to be pinned in above the row of labeled fingerprints. *What it all added up to—if it added up.* "You collect evidence," he recalled one of his professors saying, years ago, "you build your case—but something slips through your fingers, you feel like there's something missing, or there are actual clues you lack, or it's just that the evidence you do have is circumstantial . . . . What you have hold of is always, in short, a little less than complete: there's something more—even when you seem to have it all, confession, video of the perp in the act, the *works* . . . —something escapes." He looked at his watch: the heat of the room, the droning voice . . . —despite the three cups of coffee, his eyes begin to shut. "The narrative meant to arrest the truth's only true insofar as it's failure we narrate: it's always 'The One That Got Away,' got it?" Inevitably a hand went up, someone wanted to know if this would be on the test. The report should include the actual bottle or broom handle, he muses, not just a list of items forced

Q. What do you call this?

A. I use the same term the sculptor did, *oiseau*, a bird.

Q. What makes you call it a bird, does it look like a bird to you?

A. It does not look like a bird but I feel that it is a bird, it is characterized by the artist as a bird.

Q. Simply because he called it a bird does that make it a bird to you?

A. Yes, your Honor.

Q. If you see it on the street you never would think of calling it a bird, would you? If you saw it in the forest you would not take a shot at it?

Witness: No

So, if you don't want him to know how much you like him, or that you feel empty and insecure, don't call him . . . . Not calling will leave him desiring you more, make him want to see you again and call you again. It prevents him from getting to know all about you too quickly and

Dried blood in the matted, dull, dirty blond hair (instructions: hair, *dirty blond*); the skin a cold blue-gray; glazed green-brown eyes, half open, fixed: everything about her ruined, finished, over. Shall we say she appears, her hair in waves? Swimming languidly toward the viewer? *I was afraid the murdered woman would rise to help me in my search . . . .* Her scent floods the office; her teeth are like pearls, her eyes are like

"Are we then to say things like this: 'To marry is to say a few

She wakes on the beach, the sound of a woman sobbing
She wakes on the beach, shivering, drenched, a woman sobbing so close
She wakes on the chill damp sand wishing that sobbing would just

Q. Do you hold a certificate as an artist?

A. I don't know of any such

It starts with a couple of souvenirs, a handbag, a watch, and moves to the skull (wouldn't it be great to have a skull?!) and the next thing you know the desire is for a skeleton, complete. And then? How can you know what might turn out to be important later, he asks sleepily: How does anyone ever decide what to put in, what to leave out

A. Not on that object itself, on various phases of

"'Stabbed to death'? 'Tortured'? 'Mutilated'?" His laugh is perhaps a touch shrill. "'Found dismembered in . . . ' —where was it? A shallow grave . . . ?" The medical examiner clutches his brow, "But we can't be talking about the same body, much less the same case! She took an overdose of barbituates and then drank a bottle of vodka; she deliberately leapt to her death; she put her head in the oven to bake it like a cake, only she forgot to light the gas." He giggles. "The music she hoped someone would get angry or concerned about (she wanted to be found!) just wasn't, finally, in *that* neighborhood, loud enough. It's suicide—no contest." His eyes narrow slightly and his tone is more urgent: "Of course she was after a particular emotional result, part of which was—no doubt—regret, remorse. Well, all I can say is that personally *I* wouldn't

Q. What is it?
A. Because I liked it

He keeps one hand on the telephone as he reads, willing it to ring one more time, just once. The murderer could taunt him with another obscure passage from some forgotten work. Or there would be a silence and the sound of what he thought was someone breathing and then the word "indistinguishable" in brackets. Or the victim could be crouched in a phone booth by the side of the coast highway, trying to remember the number he gave her, sobbing so hard he doesn't understand what she's trying to admit. She might want to go back, or forget, maybe she wants to try to say again it was an accident. It *was* an accident. *But that did not explain how so many bodies had been reduced to such few and totally unrecognizable fragments.* The phone stays silent, he picks it up just to check the connection—there's nothing wrong with the equipment, of course. He's going over the report again, looking for something he says he'll know when he finds it. Where the truth flickers, singeing existence. "Where," he writes in the margin, "there's smoke there's smoke." The warm black handset under his palm, he mutters "Ring, ring, ring . . . " like a mantra. He's realizing that the binder's completely inadequate to the task of containing the evidence as he's beginning to conceive it. He smiles ruefully: a set of matched luggage, perhaps? To hold her arms (for instance), because they were cut off just above the elbows. No description could do it justice, but would the bones be enough? Do we need the actual injured flesh? He imagines the mechanical voice interrupting them, warning that the connection would be broken and insisting on the cost. *Where would you go if you had to leave in a hurry, what would you take?* No one, he thinks, could make sense of it in this form—it isn't fair to ask. "I see her teetering down a dim corridor swathed in filmy layers of black, trying each door in turn and I know exactly how her dark gloves flutter ineffectually at the frosted glass." Who wrote this? he writes. The silence on the other end of the line stretches out. It could be her after all this time; it's unlikely but possible: kneeling on the cold cement floor, blood-smeared, gritty with sand—whispering into the abraded plastic of the dangling handset in a graffiti-covered booth at the very edge of

Mr. _____: I object to the world of art.

Justice _____: Limit it to his own knowledge

Under oath he admits she'd put an ad in the paper: "If a nice man wants to meet a nice . . . ." He said she'd confessed she couldn't imagine getting married because, as she put it, she'd have to "get up at 4 a.m. to put on my make-up." Ladies and Gentlemen, have we not had enough of these black mysterious depths? They could not be identified as belonging to any of the women who had vanished. Pausing attentive at each slight alteration in the timbre of his snores, she tiptoes to the bathroom where she spends nearly two hours preparing the face he's prepared to meet. At night she steals back to bed only after he's safely asleep, her hair wound on curlers, face masked in thick cream, a long flowing gown clutched around the (*not tonight dear I have a headache*) body slick with restorative unguents. Now he says he only pretended to sleep? Said she wanted him to tie her up, said she said she wanted to be gagged and showed him how to insert the rolled strips of terry cloth, etc . . . . Shall we step out into . . . a world of light and life and beauty, all the fairer and sweeter in its contrast with those gloomy under-ocean regions through which we have been wandering? He dresses well, writes frequent notes to his lawyers, but otherwise seems distant from the events in the courtroom, showing no remorse. It's a deep wound, but not what she died of, we can be certain of that. Nothing here has been touched. "I hate the brain," he said she said: "Sometimes I see me dead in it." And walked out into the water and I swear that was the last

Q. When you say some represented a bird, does that (Exhibit 1) represent a bird to you?

A. To me it is a matter of indifference what

Salt water dripping from her gown echoes the clock's tickticktick. She lifts one fist and drops the wad of damp cash on the desk. Then she stands up and tears her dress down the front—the drenched silk parting easily—revealing taut, full breasts, the livid, goose-pimpled flesh, the gently curving belly, the water-darkened tangle of the pubic bush, long blue-veined thighs. She steps out of the ruined dress and, wearing only those high-heeled slippers, hoists herself onto the desk, crawling heavily over the files and photographs, through the money, between dirty glasses and cartons of coagulating take-out. Green nails glitter on the hand she's extending, clawlike. "Hey sailor," she hisses, "Hey there

In feeling it reminds me

"Dried blood in the matted, dyed, dirty-blond hair," he reads, flipping at random through the pages, "ligature marks on the wrists, hypostasis stains, the skin cold blue-gray . . . eyes, half open, fixed . . . . " He closes his bloodshot eyes; he rubs both hands hard down the sides of his unshaven face as though he would remove it like a mask. It's no bedtime story but he can't even read a couple of pages or look at the pictures again without wanting to go back to sleep. It's the silent phone, or the hours he's been keeping, the airless office, muggy gold western light cooking the dust on the half-shut blinds behind which a trapped fly bounces against the glass: buzz thwonk buzzzz thwonk zzzz

A.   If he called it a fish I would call it a fish

THE EVIDENCE

Seeps and wilts. All we have left of it. The beginning of a story: "The road slick with gore," or that's the end of it. A character appears: "Ah, summer . . . . " Beside the road the various decaying remainders of some mistimed desire. And fear. In the headlights they stop there. So swerve. The essay, as if from some distance. Or the middle of a story, in motion, a *murder mystery*: try to stay there.

The wind of our passing in their fur.
(Ruffles their fur so that for a moment they might appear to be moving.)

"I like summer, the long slow open days . . . . " Who could trust her: our character? She doesn't really want to say what she's saying (so swerve). In the left lane, beside though not yet quite passing, but I couldn't move over, I came upon too swiftly (it was night) and had to drive through the dismembered remains of a deer—I remember—the scattered chunks of bloody flesh and the road slick with gore. Try to change the ending. Try to change the ending earlier.

Windows open to the warm air

(In which anything, or so we tell ourselves, is still possible.)
As though they were merely sleeping there.

That they are the evidence of our urge for speed is an essay not a story hence unfair. The essay is always unfair. The narrative is their arrival and ours at the same place (it could almost be anywhere along the regular, the recognized, trajectories) and the same time, which is always now. But what if a story refuses to bloom there, to recall, to reanimate the fragments left after. Only at home in the mirror. Imagine her married. She straightens her shoulders, she straightens, as though someone might be watching, her shoulders.

We look at them like that and try to imagine what they were.

Only at home in the mirror where I look "tired." Maybe the story was one about, oh, whether or not to enter a kind of agreement, a contract. Dog or Fox? Cow or Deer? The essay would be making the relationship too clear, even more clear. In summation. In summer. "The ease with which the highway appears to lie over the landscape across which it travels, like a heavy ribbon . . . . " No trace of the damage done to set it so gracefully there (there, there . . .). Unless where the road narrows to one lane suddenly, by the side of the road the sight of the metal claw dropping into the earth or a truck groaning slowly away full of rocks or the dull sheen on the heavy dirt-smeared cylinder . . . . Stop there. Proceed slowly. Rolling the dust down flat into the future. Packing it down into what can be traveled, there.

So she's a student? I don't know, the pieces of her past so strewn and scattered; say she was a student: the effect, anyway, for so long, lingers. Bent over another useless essay unless summer, "the long slow open days," marked by the proliferation of bodies, in the margin or the center. Slight swerve. How long ago the realization that that was just like the space in which one first practiced a careful tracing of what were at first merely shapes, difficult, and then (capital and lower case) letters. The lower-case letters—

We remember, speeding—

Only came up to the broken line in the center. *A a, B b*. Cat or Opossum? Ripped open by a gone fender. Rubricated manuscript or book the heat bears down on—all the force of its intellect, you'd say, or its imagination—studies, and the text comes alive? The long days, to which all secrets are given up. *C c*. The pencil thick and unwieldy, grasped in a fist, it wouldn't do as bid and was, I suddenly recall, they warned us, dangerous. Amazing what you remember when you're stuck. We were not to lick the point—had I thought of licking the point? Our character as a little girl carries the freshly sharpened instrument loosely, point down, walking back to her seat, as though not sure it wouldn't bury itself by itself where they told her it could lodge and do most harm: in her eye or her mouth, or in someone else's eye or mouth.

Often they seem completely unharmed.
(In the long interstices, which are by definition nowhere.)

Exactly half the size of the former, the repetition in miniature, the offspring. So one learned to chew—to put into one's mouth if one had to and leave the impress of the teeth there—the end with the eraser. Imagine her married or with children, as they say, "of her own." When you couldn't think of the answer. Still arguing miles away, dog or coyote, if, whether, from the swift glimpse of dark blood and drab fur. I haven't forgotten her. Say again, "I haven't forgotten her."

Or a part of the road or almost

A part of the road, they've lain so still so long there.

The impressions blurred.

"What I did with my summer . . . . " I opened up the journal—somewhere between the story and the essay—to seek a certain passage there. So swerve. Quote if you have to. What you can't remember. Sneaking the cool white minty library paste into her mouth on the tip of the tongue depressor. If we weren't supposed to eat it, why was it flavored? The description of a visit to a psychic, some gone summer; her predictions of the past which was the future. Evidently a "spiritual block" in our character. A vacation. A dab on the blank facing page just inside the cover and then a due date slip could be secured.

> I'd meant or been meaning to add, since the beginning, a note on the road kill: parts of bodies, whole bodies, the road slick with gore, the air thick with the sweet stench of skunk for some distance and then the ragged tuft of skunk tail in the dark blotch of guts in the center; raccoon or squirrel on the road's shoulder, curled fetal in on themselves or smashed open in a posture of surrender to the unctuous crows in their gleaming black coats, who stalk stiffly away from the corpse and back into the tall grasses, disturbed in their ruminations by the fluster. In the rear-view mirror I saw them come back out. Their attentions to the headless bloated body of a deer. Or something nameless. Black

sponge and ashen pelt. The swollen or torn remains often no longer legible, identifiable, except as evidence. Sometimes on the asphalt nothing but a sticky, rust-colored smear.

Other students having already been there. Transeunt. Our character counting back, April by April, unable to sleep; twenty-five times and then a vagueness: each one in a different place. Wind leafing through the toll receipts. The truth if it's . . . , if it's—what? Oh Christ, she said, laughing but shaking her head, *shape*. Mrs. Wolff, teaching us about evolution, leaned on a desk, her fist—knuckles down, thumb out to the side, taking her weight (a habitual gesture)—suddenly an ape's. In the long afternoons the sky going gray, "scattered" thunderstorms. Oil-stained concrete, the sky . . . (by *shape* meaning *likeness*).

Anxiously I picked up the instrument.

We tell ourselves whatever we have to
In order not to have to stop.

But it goes on anyhow without agreement, without consent. The smell of new books that was the smell in part and as then unknown of the acid in the paper. Oh, she loved the resistance in their spines. They opened their dark shades above the struck. There would have been a time when the squirming figures making their way across the white meant nothing, then a voice made a sound in the air which hovered, and a finger, finally, isolated one of the writhing characters and pecked and pecked and pecked. Where invention and memory meet. The sound of the road going on in what seems like arrival's silence; a single feather caught between the wiper's blade and the windshield's glass. Imagine she kept a journal to help her forget.

Now.

And equally, on either side, the distances: the emptiness the event makes appear around itself. The wings of their own torn flesh. (So change the ending.) (Earlier.) Legs open, the road slick, the sound of whatever it was—the vacuum—they were using to suck (a wet noise) the dismembered body out. The red bucket. The "truth." I wrote for days, in fragments (the local anesthetic), of what, I didn't know, to arrive at or find myself in the middle of this. So reverse. All we have left. A chill breeze through the long corridor fluttered the edge of her paper dress. Our character, exit after exit. I leaned my head back, eyes shut. In her hands, insisted on and unopened, volume one of the *Remembrance* . . . . In a pause between movies (it was the night before)—the VCR on rewind, the television off—he put his hand on my stomach and, leaning close to the invisible life we'd decided to end, began slowly to recite the alphabet.

FORENSICS

"Forensics is so true."
—Gertrude Stein

The corpse is angry, *"Of course it's angry: whaddya 'spect?"* A thin curtain of flies lifts, wavers, resettles a lacy simmer across the still figure and what, after all, *did* you

Among this confusion of excuses and apologies, half-murmured as in sleep

She glances at the clock again and reads a little further: "He took her in his arms . . . ," sighs, marks the place, gets up heavily. If you listen you might hear her (out in the kitchen now, beginning to prepare dinner): it seems she wants to be heard, staging her unhappiness. But it's real, despite the staging. It might be—in part—a call for help . . . but a call already tainted with resentment or exasperation: you're always *too late.* "She felt the strength in those hands as they closed about her . . . . " She shut the book, stomped into the kitchen, dropped a pan as if to call attention to her activity, her service. I thought she was faking or at least exaggerating that clumsiness to make me, what? Help her? Pity? Identify with? She wanted me on her side but—beyond the trick of a shared grievance—was there no way to arrange that? One woman is dead, another's in danger, but, smart or plucky, *she'll* be saved in the nick of time! In the novel her life is so thrilling the heroine never wastes any time *reading* about

Talk of depths! We are in them at last, and no mistake. Down—down! Deeper and deeper! Above our heads are piled three or four miles of water, and the pressure upon our unfortunate bodies is

She lay down. She went to bed early but it wasn't just that. She 'took to her bed.' She lay down more often in the middle of the day, not to sleep but to be left alone, to take up again the threads of an absorbing plot. She brought the books home by the armload, stacked them on her nighttable, on the floor by her side of the bed, in piles a foot or so deep: skulls and guns and daggers, spilled bottles of pills or poison, broken necklaces on the gleaming dustjackets, the broad-shouldered shadow of a man in a doorway, a woman fleeing in moonlight. She lay there, smoking, twisting a lock of hair, eyes on the page, anxious. I only came to say I was going out. Reluctantly she looked up. Married for the third time to a man who, it seemed, had disappointed her: bitter, impatient, grieving, jealous, she said Yes, I could, *but*. She had a daughter who hovered in the doorway as ferocious judgment, barely awaited permission—and vanished. The book came back up: on the cover an enlarged fingerprint, a bloody knife, the body of the

On that strip of exposed beach beside the highway long slender veils of semi-transparent wet mist tear, shiver, and reform in a shifting tableau of strange, half-remembered shapes. A thick smear of blood on the glass wall of the phone booth turns black in the glare of the

The corpse struggles to its knees, what you thought was the corpse, and—muttering to itself—starts scrubbing at the bloodstains. It's too late to offer to help her, clearly. She says, *Well, to tell you the truth*

Covered by slime that immobilizes the anemone's stinging mechanism, the damselfish snuggles safely in deadly arms. As if in payment for its haven, it lures other fish into the[1]

---

1. She has to choose correctly between two men: one of the men wants her to be happy, the other wants her dead; it isn't clear which is which (until almost the last page we won't know which is which). Needless to add that each of them is, in their own way, compellingly attractive.

Try to desire, he suggests sternly, something more than reassurance, more than

A stranger hands over a faded snapshot of other strangers sitting near the seaside: a "family reunion," right? Improvised arrangement so that everyone, kneeling in front of the beach chairs or standing, fits. Children and the seated elderly in front. "Remember?" "Yes. Yes, of course." And then a sidelong glance to see if this was what was expected, as in, Did I get it right, or what happens next? Another photograph with no apparent connection to the first, and yet it seems it's crucial also to 'remember' this. Another lineup. What can memory mean in this context? Shutting her eyes, rubbing the sides of her face as if to loosen a mask. What does it mean, to *remember* . . . . Meanwhile a surf of glossy images dealt as swiftly as they're taken back: "And what about *this* one?" "And this?" "What about

---

She reluctantly marks her place in that more glamorous life before getting up to make dinner. I can hear the creak of the bedsprings as she gets up. In the book she's reading everything depends—oh, say it's all taking place on the Costa del Sol: the emerald water, that astonishing light . . . —on which man she chooses to turn to for help. She leaves the book lying face up on the bed: the lurid cover (*The Body on the Beach*) catches my eye as I follow her into the kitchen to ask what I can do, hearing a clatter of dishes meant, I thought, to tell me she wanted help or that it wasn't fair if I went on reading, since . . . . I'm not sure either of us notices where we are or what we are doing: frowning out at an imagined line of white breakers or rotting bodies below the author's expensively researched red sandstone cliffs. Two men, both handsome and strong and smart and . . . —which to trust? Roberto and Ethan, Abdul or Josh, stock figures more real to us than the kitchen in which a mother and daughter are working together saying only those words necessary for the accomplishment of the despised, necessary task. The warm, slowly dimming sunlight glinting on the washed lettuce; an avocado—from the tree in the backyard—opening smoothly under the knife to reveal velvety green flesh and the brown polished globe of the pit . . . —it's worthless. The moment has no beauty or meaning either woman can possibly recognize, shut as they are to each other, furious at this *interruption*. But the stories they left are only the most obvious sign in an elaborate system the function of which is apparently to advertise what must not be confessed: that the possibility of happiness had been or was being removed from this life, set out of reach of that ambitious girl, in transit, already wanting always something else. As for the mother, banging a platter down on the counter, pouring another shot of gin over the melting ice in her glass—abandoned, by definition an *elsewhere*, a past tried and false, entrance as exit, discarded skin or self—she can't

Optimum distance from which to have viewed the perpetrator: 2–12 feet

For a long time the mother goes to bed early: right after dinner she takes her coffee back to the bedroom, she's "tired." Her husband or children do the dishes (because she, we are reminded, *cooked* . . .). In the book she can't wait to get back to, another body's been discovered. The cover gleams: there's a picture of coiled rope or spilled white tablets, a broken necklace, a phone off the hook, a bloody[2]

But what is it she—never satisfied—checks the actual against? What is the gauge (one suspects it's constantly changing: that there's no one "it") against which the actual, always measured, always lacks? If this life is in need of revision, correction, adjustment (but one wonders if the "lost" blueprints to which she compares the finished work ever existed: one begins to wonder if the template's not a myth), the little touches she finds so necessary only destabilize the fragile stuff, evidently, as each action calls forth a further series of equally necessary actions: each revision opening up a possible further revision—until there's suddenly a thousand or so it seems insufficient ways of proceeding any one of which might[3]

---

2. Some chapters are little more than a list of the names of sitcoms and late-night movies the family watched; others detail the endless leftovers, note which cupboards the scrubbed pots are returned to, chart the gradual erasure of the evidence. In the morning she's up before dawn and already—by the time we join her for the stiff and frankly unbelievable dialogue—fretful, unhappy, weary. Endless mugs of bitter coffee and cheap cigarettes and the journal she hunches over, mouth set, a fierce grip on the pen, something hopeless already in the effort at

3. Each 'truth,' told, seems to stand in briefly, inadequately, for what already escapes: sign in the air for X behind which X (shooting, as the squid does, between itself and the threatening eyes of the other, a ghost of ink, translucent double as distraction, hanging in the water, already beginning to disperse) vanishes

The echoing vague empty hallway—each door shut—a dull, underwater light sieved through the chipped gilt letters floating across the grayish glass. Silence in which she writes "I'm desperately sad." Or, "I am a lost spirit." And then nothing after

Gaping windows in roofless houses full of dark water. On the invisible strings of chill currents the dead are jerked into some parody of life like drunken puppets. In and out they go, the drowned, hurried, tugged toward various missed appointments, reeling back through the doorless threshold, to topple on the broken steps. They sway on the ruined landing as if about to speak, slightly surprised or despairing, faces disconnected from the strange slow gestures their bodies make. They stagger toward each other and, without touching, fall past, slip through the other's grasp: their hands reach out and drift awkwardly, empty, back. They shuffle from foot to foot as if ashamed, not sure what to do, where to go next. All of this in the most extraordinary of silences: so dense with what hasn't been said, what needs to be said, what should have been said, so loud with what you still think are secrets you can't[4]

I wanted to know who you were, really.[5] I wondered if you'd ever been happy.

---

4. *Approach her, if at all, where language falls apart, where you (in the crying woman you see them seeing you as as you rise to go) fall apart. In the failure, in the deep shame. As though I had done nothing with my life. Approach (by turning away) the wasted hours in which we attempted, ineffectually, some awkward approximation of happiness. You could call long distance, but you don't. The implication here—that it's too late—is, confess, weeping messily, false. Approach in the admission that you have no idea where or how to start. Take the silence (broken by banalities, the barest cautious signalings of a distrustful, fragile truce) you've settled for and test it, keep testing it. Stop dreaming of happy endings, answers, a rest*

5. She looked up from the book she was reading: corpses littered every page, almost. She went to the kitchen, her shoulders tense, her mouth small, a scowl on her face. We had to ask what we were eating—a sour odor rose in the steam from the uncovered dish—they had to remind us children were starving in . . . well, the location shifted. Drying on the sea-green plate, greasy

I wanted to know what your life was like before us. In answer to my request that you write something of what you remembered, first an incoherent flurry of apologies and worries about money and then at last

Words occur: *abandoned, betrayed, drowned, lost* . . . . Words that break across and over, flow backwards and away without changing or disentangling, only slightly shifting the stuff churned up by their repetitive passage. "This makes sand." I can feel the imprint of my feet in the tide's drag as a raised shadow, resisting erosion. What should be sad here? In the mirror the woman measures the increasing graininess in the loosening skin of her neck again as if distrust would help. She won't talk, her eyes restless and frightened and furious. The slightly gritty texture of

---

continents of fork-printed mush. Sometimes the news on TV during dinner, but mostly we must have talked to each other: what did we talk about? The murderer wanted to know the truth: how things looked "on the inside"; he liked to listen to his victim's stomachs, to their hearts. We waited to be "excused" from the table. In early anatomy illustrations the dead often reach down and part their own flesh, exposing secrets they seem no longer impressed by or still can't face. He rests his head, for a moment, gently, on the chest of the boy he handcuffed. Because I was a woman, she said, *You'll see, you'll have to learn to cook, you'll have to* . . . . My brother learned to stay out of the sound of her voice: he came in, ate, joked around, left. A flayed body holds up its own skin, in one illustration, for instance: slack ghost on which the exposed muscles of the face still manage to cast a disdainful look, holding up in the other hand that sharp knife. Always leftovers—to put away in carefully marked containers, to encounter again in indescribable casseroles and bitter soups; even the sodden, wilted salad was saved. The roar of the dishwasher filled the house: like being in a car wash. She went back to her book, but nervously, as she read she chewed the edges of her fingers until they bled. Her nicotine-stained thumb crusted over with a blackish scab the shape of her teeth. He put the bodies in an acid bath. How did the night pass? We must have had homework. Her seethe of continued worry behind descriptions of coastline and hairline, lists of evidence and suspects, brittle intricacies of plot. Hours had to be killed, consciousness had to be put off, for what? The murderer speaks of how his victims were first an image, then a symbol, at last a problem, and finally a *threat*. We might see the writer as attempting to reverse this trajectory. He was fascinated by the unwilled gurgles and murmurs and thumpings; he wanted a lover alive but completely obedient. I imagined she was waiting for me to grow up, to get out of the house, to set her free. He called them his tragic products. "The victim is the dirty platter after the feast," the murderer writes. I thought I had ruined her life . . . ; or I thought I thought that to justify *removing* myself

the skin as though she were turning into dust, a corpse seen through layers of crime tape, through the morgue's plastic wrap, reconstructed from the details he couldn't forget after the endless amount of time spent going over and over the photographs. Imagining words he might have meant, as on some sheets whose pattern resembled nothing so much as a fence or net, to say as he enters her—repeatedly. That's the word: "enters." It actually happened, of course. But not (ever) exactly like

A gray day, into which everything vanishes: bleached sky and ocean, fog-blurred beach, swift flash of pale foam and

The corpse sits up—what you thought was the corpse—and, with some difficulty, smooths away the possibly telltale footprints of her would-be assassin (but the sand is so vague, who would even think to read them as "footprints"?) as far as she can reach with the arm he didn't break: a frown. She says *If you can't say anything* nice

They take the body into the surf and wash it off; they haul it back up above the tide line, already arguing about how it looked: *No, it wasn't like* that! Each one remembering some slightly differing detail, certain of what they recall, each with a clear picture of how it was supposed to go; how it went. Positioned, one insists, lying down himself—legs spread—to describe it, exactly like that . . . . Someone else practices falling forward, how would you land if you had been running, or if your arms had been raised in surrender or defense . . . . Maybe, one of them finally admits, *We shouldn't have . . . in the first place* . . . . But it's much too late to argue the finer points of action versus

How could I have done that? I am very sad. My spirit is sad, lost. Paints are gone, I cannot afford new and now clay is gone—I miss that, too. Do not have the strength and energy to do clay any more. For many years the creative work was what I did, who I was—and I tried many different

Seen, as sung, on a train only passing through: her eyes, how familiar, et cetera; she gave . . . / that was . . . / but she's only . . .

Perched fussily on the living room couch (she'd opened a plastic garbage bag to sit on so as not to stain the upholstery), the corpse refuses to remove the bloody dress. I'm helping her clean her nails: she's afraid she might have caught a thread from his suit there, or some skin from his wrists. I've been trying to tell her she reads too many detective novels. She sighs. She doesn't like the tentative way I'm holding her fingers, she doesn't think I'm going deep enough. *Honestly*, she says, *do I have to do* everything

Why was it necessary to imagine her like that: blurred features in the [illegible], steps echoing down an empty

Sand on the floor; window sills decked with broken shells and twisted twigs of grayish driftwood, shreds of dried sea wrack; the flattened corpse of a oil-blackened seagull on the desk, neck twisted, wings spread over the sodden pages of the unfinished report; reek from an upended crab shell on a file cabinet; shattered fragments of traps and buoys in the wet carpet among blue-green bits of beach glass. He likens his mother's mode of speech to the waves: "The way she'll say something and then take it back immediately." Small waves, coming and going on that little strip of rocky beach where his father spoke in 'objective' assertions: not "I liked the book," but "It's a good book." On the phonograph, needle deep in a scratch, caught sop of polluted surf: *kershps kershps kershps*

As though to say a few words. As though I didn't kill her. As if

Trying to make the technique itself as close to the ocean's as I could get it: going over and over the thing, saying it, taking it back, pushing it up as an instant's offering—at the tide line, script of seaweed, shells and stones, sand dollars, trash, foam scum. Written on the shifting stuff in the swift shine of the wet already vanished . . . ; "Speaking," Levinas writes, "implies a possibility of breaking off and

She keeps saying she isn't mad at me, really, it's her murderer: *What a mess*, she snaps. Holding the gaping wound closed with one hand she's picking up the crushed cigarette butts, the burnt matches, the cufflink, the torn page from his address book . . . . I've been trying to tell her to let me do this: she should really get some rest. She waves me away, too furious even to look up, hissing, *Maybe he wants to be arrested, if this is the best*

"Clumsier each year, more awkward, more distrustful of yourself, more—but it seemed increasingly turned inward—furious. I was also angry for those wrong, awkward, ragged, incomplete, sad gestures, for the silences you used to signify your displeasure—or so I thought—and the sudden bursts of angry, tearful, self-pitying speech, for the fragility you seemed to flaunt, for your constant need of my approval (when you weren't, alternately, actively attempting my diminishment); I must've been terrified I would become you, and attained, of course, in that terror, a certain likeness. You got up from the dinner table for no reason, seized on each chance to be hurt, on any remark you could turn into an insult; you made a scene—the untouched food cooled on our plates. You set the glass down hard, you drew yourself up and said every word of what suddenly seemed to you to be the necessary truth. I've forgotten what you said, most of it. You suspected me—admit it—of every horror: once I could recite the long list. Wrong about most of it, you were right to suspect there were few lengths I wouldn't have gone to escape you, to escape what you promised was also my future (you said 'wait and see,' with a laugh that ravaged your face). You asked for pity, flaunting my fate: that body becoming heavy and graceless and fragile, every impulse doubted, thwarted or false. But the evident, unceasing, desire for an admiration I couldn't give you was the worst part: I felt how I failed and drew back, kept drawing back, adding failure to failure, increasing the distance. Trying now—in this writing—to get closer, I'm just making a mess: failed, ugly, unwieldy, incomplete . . . . What, I keep wondering, could I have admired? What did you do well? Of what I knew or had been told mattered? In my memory every gesture seems tight, fraught, acted out theatrically as evidence of how you were oppressed: slamming the shovel into the earth, grinding the point of the pen against the page, burning a black crust on the bottom of the pan, as if to make us all sorry . . . . 'Cooking isn't fun,' you sneered, 'but you'll have to learn to do it!' Because I was a woman, I would also be trapped (but you wanted children, you insist). I'd be sorry, you said. I'd see. I keep trying to say how it was, but I'm afraid of us both. Days go by without a word—then I'm back at these notes: You had silences, sudden rages, you said things behind our backs or screamed at us, huge, bewildering emotions attached to something behind the words I couldn't see or reach. We were bad, we were good, were loved—or not. You had one of your headaches. We had to be quiet. Some mistake brought it all down in a crash. Couldn't we see we were in the way, that we stood between you and happiness, you . . . and your art. Your 'creativity.' First you painted, then it was enamels, then photographs, for awhile you wrote, then it was weaving, or ceramics . . . . You only needed the right equipment, you said, though mostly, once you had it—the husband you often seemed to despise bought what he could of what you said you absolutely had to have—you stopped. There was an ongoing story—about illness fatigue pain fear anger lack of money and nothing ever being right—in which we all seemed stuck. From a few clues you dropped about your life before us, from the evidence in your jewelry box and stuffed in the back of your closet, I invented a past for you I tried to inhabit: you would have been happier without us, I guessed. (When I at last understood what the ongoing feeling of queasiness meant I scheduled the abortion at once.) Now your bewildered attempts to be supportive of what must seem my mysterious life. I write as if one could untangle roles, actions . . . . You, you, you: I point. Is it necessary to say this, to leave 'a record' (even if flawed and necessarily inaccurate)? To stand up, saying what has to be said until tears interrupt? In the heavy silence we lift our forks again, bring the chilled food to our lips despite our tight, our aching throats. Uneasily in the interstices some 'truth' sways, suspended, still evolving, infinitely distant from the phrases: 'She didn't love us, she didn't love herself . . . . ' You, I. Far from insight these unsteady revelations, these residual enactments. 'I believed it was my fault.' It should be possible finally to say something—to sum it all up, to be done with it, finished. But the ongoing attempt's apparently all that's possible: coming forward, drawing back, incomplete sentences breaking against an unstable subject they shift, dissolve and

GRAVIDA LOCA

She trips into my office in the middle of a story she says she knows I've heard at least a hundred times she's sure I won't believe she says can't wait. *Cut to the chase.* She leaned over the desk asking me to . . . . An angry grief dismembers all it comes in contact with: the corpse forbids certain gestures, genre fumblings, fingers tentative at what you know you know: *Can't you do* anything *right?* A story she says the twists and turns of she'd bet anything are already as familiar to me as . . . , but, "You can't experience your own interior by closing your eyes and concentrating on it." My face almost in the smooth abyss between her breasts—her words blurred—I watched a vein pulsing in her throat. That self-conscious breathiness a trick she'd worked hard to perfect: you had to—to hear her—lean closer so even the most mundane remark became intimate. I don't remember what she said, it's as though the sensation is blunted, or there's only the ghost of a feeling . . . . something I'd read once; I was trying to calm her down, saying *Yes, yes.* She didn't have to ask: I made her every promise in the book the minute she came through the door in that glittering, low-cut dress, the reflected lights in her hair, her long-lashed eyes already half shut . . . . *You don't know what love is,* she said. "In order to discover your own contents you have to investigate the inside of someone else." And then I was standing beside the body, another useless witness. As if with a check list: every limited, stupid promise of the limited, stupid realist . . . . I didn't do anything but try to talk to her. I don't make this shit up. Early in the morning: under marquees still advertising last night's enticements, the pale manager hosing down the sidewalks turns the stream of water away for a moment as you pass (at your feet in the force of the current, cigarette butts, condoms, a needle, ticket stubs, the cap off a fifth, etc.), and a bleak exhalation of spilled booze, stale smoke, dried cum, and the ammonia they're scrubbing the whole thing down with comes out of the dark entrance like a dead breath. I lit another cigarette off the butt of the first. Outside the scene, one of the team being violently sick at the sight of what was left. In fact I *am* trying to remain aware of the entire action of which I can only represent a moment. Someone suggested I lie down in the chalk outline myself. "She trips into my office": for me it starts there ("beautiful, alive, desperate"), for her it began somewhere else, that mechanism which delivers her violated remains later as symptom and excuse. I swear I could feel her impatience ripening into disgust. *Just touch me, please, confidently, as though you knew what you were doing, just* . . . . Now around the body the furtive experts, their handkerchiefs pressed to their mouths, their snatched glances and uncertainties, their jealously hidden, spidery notes: "Remember." Breakfast rising hot and sour, also, in *my* throat. What would they have done if she'd come to them (hell, maybe she had, I didn't know anything for sure yet), letting the slit skirt of that gown—as she perched on the edge of the desk with her legs crossed—slide back on one smooth pale thigh to show that there was literally *nothing* after the stocking's black lacy edge bit flesh; if she'd, leaning down (saying You're not listening to me), begged in a harsh whisper, *Your mouth* . . . . Someone rushed in with the shocking intelligence. Refusing to meet my eyes. I can just imagine them sighting up the line of "creamy" "silken" skin—*describing,* as if

"I let them," the painter insisted, "relax into the pose which most suits them" (this in translation, in reference to those bodies torqued to get the most from each curve, twisting to display the convex surfaces up to the gaze, to the light)—a laugh. Imagine a figurine you could point to to speak of the afflicted area, so as to not have to take your clothes off: ivory, the open box lined with silk. As in, "Of course I'll still be here when you get back": not a question but a sentence, as if to have just decided, all by herself, to lie down a moment, one arm behind her head, eyes shut. *I can close my eyes.* "Remember, it was the *possession* of this desired thing, which was, in itself—the very act of assuming possession was a very antisocial act—giving expression to this person's need to *seize* something that was . . . uh, uh, highly valued, at least on the surface, by society." I can close my private eyes. No rip in the illusion's surface brutally introducing itself, anxious to confess, to say, Here's what we were seeing all along, or something like, Here's what seeing does to what it sees: here's what looking looks like—watch. A sticky, sweet, salt-scented heat, and the waves bringing down a gavel, thump, thump, thump: another life sentence. They hustle her away, as if there was only one corpse: stolen off to the other scenes she needs to steal: "You can't keep her here forever." Limbs sprawled or strained into a presentation of *joie-de-vivre en plein aire*: the shallow grave in the forest, the dump site in front of the waterfall behind the broken factory wall. Sublime—no picnic. Ravaged by wildlife. The experts turn the tape recorder off, pause to wonder again how to ask for the instant it's always too late to ask for: the instant of . . . trust . . . . Good cop again? Or is it time to try bad cop? *I want to close my eyes, I just want to rest.* She would be (re)moved or fade livid into the colorless beach as if left too long under a developer's light, or, with a pallet knife and a damp cloth she as wet paint—the *key,* the only, witness—would be scraped off. Another flesh-colored blob, toothy bright red gape of open lips and cartoon breasts or

"This might give us one clue as to why this person returned to that site on at least several occasions. Perhaps it was discovered that when a body was left there, and later when the individual would return to check out the situation, [he] would find it was no longer there! And concluded

"The feminine form." Nothing for it. I *had* heard that story. Naked, of corpse—I mean *course*. Where "out of fear or out of whatever" she capitulates, following instructions. He pretended to be a cop, nightstick following the curve, note, of the buttock from the shallow indentation where the spine . . . . (But where did one part stop—and the next . . . ?) Arc of thigh, sharp angle of the lifted arm bent so as to protect the face. The graceful lines of. (Suddenly anxious to demarcate specific areas: This is where that [named section] of the body starts, and this . . . . Cunt, for instance, ass.) "I'd like to assert that we're held, if not by the formality of the composition, then by the coldness of the values—at some distance from what we are seeing, from what, in fact, we apparently want—are supposed to want—to watch: the emphasis is on connections made intellectually." If it weren't for the way the body's been divided up by inked-in lines telling where to cut and the name of each

But a severed head, he reminded us, weighs more than you think. At which point

"We are attracted only to the darkness of others' lives, never our own." True or false? These stills spilled out on the dust-covered desk don't even *belong* to the case. The case (as per several recent official reminders) only one in a series of disappearances: no connection with these almost pornographic images, dubiously acquired by a highly unreliable source. That they found their way into the files at all is proof—as if any more were needed—of a lack of fit between me and my work: lately I'm just not myself. *He removed their teeth after death so that he could use their mouths* . . . . Darkness does "fall," evidently: nothing stays where you put it. Illustration: the curtain of flesh over the abdomen parted to reveal, in the shadowed womb, the exposed fetus shielding its face. *Why, I'll speak to it*—apology after apology. Only once

Turning up his collar against the wind sheer off the tide's wash, muttering his borrowed motto: "Exactitude is not truth." Smashed in the wreckage (he writes) of the boat, the body: shuttled through the complex rigging as sail, as shroud, arms woven into the ropes (he notes), the flesh perhaps never so obviously little more than a garment, what little was left, summoned by the suitors: police photographer, medical examiner, the team from forensics, members of the press held off behind the tape, the whole scene "bathed" in harsh floodlights, every grain of sand distinct, the chief down by the surf's edge the dragged inscription of the broken keel leads back to: *crying*, as the cliché has it, *his eyes out*—that also goes in the report. Eyes hacked out, sockets licked clean, tongue cut. Tangled in the net, like a broken puppet (he writes), holes in each palm as though meant to be strung up, as if it were there you'd attach whatever the puppet should appear to be holding, to 'carry' onstage and off, its props: things to be grasped in hands that can't. (These notes worked over, endlessly reworked.) The stiff position's rebroken, once again the rigor's forced. The similes snatched from that rant swept back in shreds from where someone stood sobbing into the not-quite-covering noise of the surf. But how can you ever finally know (he wrote to her, admitting that here he was again *quoting*) what to include and what

In the witness box for the umpteenth time she insists it doesn't matter. Not any longer: it was a long time ago. She's sure he didn't mean it. Her head an unsteady smear of blue, her name a list of leaks to the press. He opens her unresisting hand and on the soft flesh of her palm with red magic marker he draws a heart. Her name a civil suit. She's silent as they play the tape of the confession—it wasn't *his* fault: the overbearing mother who . . . , etc., absent father, etc., the unresponsive women, etc., and anyway, she *wanted* him to tie her up, etc., and did she think he was *made* of money, etc., etc . . . . She's silent, thinking he might still want to marry her, someday, if she's good now, if she'll *just*

"And as one single body did not suffice for so long a time, it was necessary to proceed by stages with so many bodies as would render my knowledge complete

He lifts his hands from the rubricated lines left in the soft white flesh of her neck; he steps back, in her eyes his image, dulling but still distinct. He looks over the scene with *a critical eye*. Leading up to the blot of the body the dotted line his footprints make. Has his hat, in fact, blown off—to be caught somewhere in the tangled underbrush behind the broken brick wall, just out of sight? Did he (somewhere in the elided struggle to make her cooperate) lose one of his monogrammed cufflinks? What's that clenched in her livid fist? Is this *one of his best*? A button from his coat clutched in her dead hand, a fragment of the letter insisting they need to "talk," maybe a couple of hairs (for the DNA print)? Gulls swoop close, bring back a version of the screams he stopped. Does he have, he wonders, a *style* yet? Was the murder in *his*

I wanted to know who you were, really. I wondered if you'd ever been happy. Were you always afraid of wanting what you wanted, he asks, or was it just

There's a man sitting in the late afternoon's increasing dimness, a pile of photographs spread on the desk. An open binder and a carton of take-out: crumbs soak small oil shadows into single-spaced pages of typescript, a red gout of sauce masks part of an identikit sketch. Rain and the intermittent tearing sound of tires on wet asphalt, a creaking as the emptied building settles into itself, tick of a clock. A single light on the descriptions of the suspects, "Tall but not too tall, you know, well, about your height." The list keeps getting longer, though every name has already been checked out and off. *To keep discovering—from each of the possible viewpoints* . . . . The witnesses shrug, say he looked like a lot of guys, "You know"; they choose a nose off of one picture, hesitate among eye-shapes. Looking at them as they looked, looking for the first faint sign of something like recognition. Among the citations and fragments. The witnesses argue about hair color, anxious to help. "Maybe your shade, or a little darker?" Which version do you want? "He seemed so nice, quiet, shy . . . " (etc.). "He was wearing a sort of uniform . . . . " Her open mouth full of blood, the body twisted as if

Afraid of wanting what you thought you wanted, or what you thought you *shouldn't*

Gulls hover, drop clams down onto the asphalt of the empty parking lot. Pale grasses, where the dunes start, glitter in the last of the light. It's late. The surface of the water, wind-roughened, thrusts up and smashes down in icy shards. Everyone else has left, only our detective insists on waiting, anxiously copies that crude sketch in the sand into his notebook, exaggerating boobs and hips. "I'm just," he says, drawing a deep "x" where the abdomen would be, "trying. To get at the . . . truth. Of what, actually. Happened." The paper raggedly tearing where a dark, ink-soaked area pools in the reenactment. The tide goes out, the sand bar begins to reappear, scattered birds strut the gleaming blue-black banks of mussels. The body's discovered under the desk or behind a filing cabinet as the sun sinks slowly into the water, as he brings out the fifth of scotch. He could have done it any time in a fog like this. Another few minutes and there wouldn't have been so much as a trace. The receding water darkens at the horizon: "wine-stained" now that we've learned to see it like

I hefted the knife in my hand. The gun, the ice-pick, whatever: the weapon, here at last, the *raison de n'être pas* as someone laughed—back in the days when it was just an academic question, when we had some *perspective*, some *distance*. How I longed to take—not the trip down memory lane the corpse had taken, but—just a few crucial steps back. In class the diagram of the body marked the site of a resurrection: whoever held still to be outlined as fallen getting quickly up, brushing off traces of chalk dust, to rejoin the spectators and experts. Who wouldn't want to lie down for a moment in the trace of a former life out of which they'd lift themselves, reciting, "Dying / Is an art, like everything else . . . "? But the thing behind me (one of the detectives tried, retching, to delimit—the chalk a wet paste in his sweaty, trembling fist . . .), seemed to insist there was no way to safely demarcate the festering past. I reopened the case: exhumed the incomplete report, questioned again the aging, forgetful witnesses, tested the accounts, went over the list of suspects, tagged and bagged the scrapbooks and photo albums, prom cards, dried flowers, souvenirs and memorabilia. Ephemera, any fragment of which might be, or point to, the fact we sought. "Because, of course," (the Professor's sonorous drone, borne on the fly buzz behind me, came back, saying *there is no such thing as trivia*, saying . . .) "of course there is some voice here saying what the self had never understood about the self, some trace in which the answer is already plain but which we are as yet untutored to read." He looked at his watch. "Dead, you are 'on time,' or 'in time,' contained at last . . . . " I rubbed my eyes, took the stub of chalk from that livid hand, saying *Hold still*, and, looking over at the corpse, marked a few points on the body I had, experimentally. "But the only thing that deserves to be called a *clue*," the Professor admonished from that classroom which lingered on in me as if it were a dream, in which a bell now rang—through which he continued his self-congratulatory murmurings, "is that detail the discovery of which *completely*

Sand packed down over the mouth I don't dare open; sand tamped down over the eyelids kept carefully shut; sand I might hear moving against itself, whispery grind of grain on grain, if I dared to move, if

HESITATION MARKS

You are to ask what the coast is called, note it down, make a landing, obtain reliable information, and, having charted the coast, return. *The Deep and the Past.*

> For about ten years he walled himself up to concentrate on the physical modeling of the sea, in all scales from a bay to a hemisphere. [His] private ocean was a circular tank thirteen feet in diameter. He could spin it up to ten revolutions per minute to create his own Coriolis effect. The surface of the tank was covered with rubber continents and oceans at an average depth of an inch and a half (representing the wind-driven layer of the actual sea). Blowers sent breezes over it, reproducing the the earth's wind system. Effects of wind could be measured by the drift of Ping-Pong balls floating on the surface and shuttlecocks suspended from thin wires overhead. He used ink and chemicals as current tracers. He used dyes that sank, others that floated so that a camera loaded with color film could follow the circulation of his tagged water masses. "It was an intriguing experiment . . . I enjoyed every minute of it. Every oceanographer yearns to hold the earth in his hand . . . . We could change conditions: we plugged up the Straits of Florida to learn what that would do to the Gulf Stream, we opened the isthmus of Panama . . . . "

Let that river be drawn full of ships to make the more show. Place by the river (mouth of the); lifted hand of the corpse. Stilled blood of. Spill of dirty blond hair. So that. Checked. No. Choked. In the shade of; as seen from behind (this). Hand over mouth, not to. Punctuated barrier. Something choked back in silence. The flow stopped. At the river's mouth, the dredge. Thick stuff languidly roiling at the salt point. A black root trailing green moss. A long flat stretch of livid sand. Fog drawn in shreds across a landscape. Hand over. From which dark figures gradually detach themselves. Focused a few steps and then again lost. Shifting wall of chill dank stuff which "swallowed them up." Where trails off. Mouth. Without exactly forgetting our grief. Proof: remembered body, headless, naked, legs spread, in one lifted hand that flickering light. *At Work At Sea.*

> When their clothing gave out, they sewed new garments from sea leopard skins, with threads of blackfish tendon and buttons of whalebone. Sea elephants furnished the leather for stout moccasins; smoking pipes were fashioned from their tusks—the hollow stems were wing bones of albatross. Purses they made from seal flippers and albatross feet. One of them lived for some time in a hut he fashioned by tilting a whale's skull against an overhanging cliff, reinforced with rafters of whalebone and roofed with sea elephant skins. They wrote their experiences with splinters of bone, using albatross gall for ink.

But numberless such adventurers have lived and died and been forgotten. Sea wrack, wreck, flotsam and so forth, residue strewn on the strand *so to speak*, the scattered stray remains of former truths, enough left to keep you thinking you might be searching in the right place or somewhere near the right place. The push and drag wears the words transparent, cracks the phrases, lifts—unsettling—the breath. Out of these traces to retrace

1. *"I'll have to"*

The beach at dawn. *A cold chill went through a sold bill sent who annulled or annealed gold spent or lent to, bent "a cold chill"—meant to*
The beach at dawn and the two of them. *In being told the damp clothes or damn close, sure—insisted on, "I want to make some $*
The woman, the man. *Goddamn I meant to go eye meant to ghost or men "to go" (real: lent to). The body disposed*
"I guess I'll have to change." *Recoiled sold, recalled as sent to: still played by the stories— beginning, middle, end—we bent to*
The fog, the glow in the haze to the east. *The moldy thrill of where it all went to: old stills, gold-value bills, the drive-thru*

2. *Silhouettes*

"I guess I have to be the one to change."
"I guess you wouldn't say so if you thought so!"

(When they meet, they seem perfect for each other. Met. Seemed. When they were perfect for each other they met, remember? Later the wear and tear as we say, the toll that time takes, is it time? Involved. In a fog that permeates. You have to be as smart and alive all the time, well, *responsive,* as though you were the writer, finding your way in a form you weren't familiar with. So introduce [again] an interference the context subdues [what is it to recognize?]: "If the word 'chack' is inserted in a sentence about poultry-raising, a proofreader is apt to misread it as 'chick.' If it appears in a sentence about banking, it will be misread as 'check.'")

Went through "a cold chill" (went through), shivered (musics): *A cold chill went through* The figures beached on the ground of. Bitched.

3. *(If you aren't going to)*

She shudders, pulls the raincoat he lent her closer around her shoulders, they begin to have shadows, maybe, the sky brightens and objects take on depth, form, color: this is the distance between them, then, and who stands here or hear murmuring quietly a sodden, icy, exhausted description, in which He leans to kiss her lightly or She puts one hand, for a moment, on his thigh. How will they recover desire? How will we? The dim light already not only enough but in fact too much to watch these diminished expectations unfold in. (But the reader warms, as warned, his or her shivering life . . . .) They collide hard in the clinch: their teeth—*ouch!*—clank together. Enough light or light enough to discern . . . . Your word for mine. *And the ashes blew toward us with the salt wind* . . . . They stand back for a moment—eyeing each other warily—holding their mouths. Another translation for the dew-bedecked stand-in, standing again unsteady on 'where once we . . . ': *dawn, waves* and *my heart* "breaking."

4. *The Deep-at-Work*

And "enough"   (went through)

(dimensions)   sent care of "A cold . . .

"Small world!"   (obsolete dimensions)

"Funny I didn't see you!"   (What they meant

> *(The window intersperses facts with sentences, which the student completes*
> *in the space provided. He actively participates, he moves at his own*
> *speed and knows at all times how well he is doing—all ideal educational*
> *practices.)*

The light is gray and fragile. Space is curved so it comes back upon itself. It's a long

time, master soleil, I have been sitting here with my notebook open, de-scribing

The *written character*   (a shallow grave)

You be whatever I to I to (you   perfect light

                                             (were

(We're they?) "I guess I gotta go back some . . . . "

                                             at an address

Still (I meant you   (deme[a]ntia)

The consoled real   (assiduous chiming)

                                             (fog and sea and so forth

"My hands are open but never clean, never empty . . . . "

                                             description: the voice

                                                at dawn, the beach:

Naming

            And here is the body

                    ("I guess I gotta go back some still . . . . ")

            And here is the body   fold or bent to

"Small world."   Begin beginning:

Naming (what love starts: mistaking a recognizable, recognized   noise—listen

(Again)—for recognition [What does it mean to

5. *I guess I halve to be the one two*

"Light enough to see her sequined dress, green, glittering like fish scales (light snagged

Or

"Caught light in the wind-rippled surface of the water as though a green sequined dress

    (The ground of our understanding and agreement eroded, or was

    shifting? The product of former erosions anyway, filling the shoes not

    ours, "like boats," slipping off as you made our / are uncertain way

    into the exasperation in her voice [she traded in her voice] in his and

    "because it is a noun you think it exists, don't you"—don't you? Who

    will *change*? Now.)

"My hands are never clean but they are empty." Engraved or set down earlier. (The

property appears first as a tool, then as a weapon, finally as a clue, or proof.) The

reader can tell from the thickness of the pages under her right thumb that everything ends soon or beautifully. Different anyhow. (The first words: naming those who were glad to be named, believing they were by that gesture loved and recognized.) Began to feel strange. I will work at becoming transparent. Feel free to open it up and let it fall apart, feel free to free from my notebook of the damned to tear these sodden, perfectly blank

I SHADOW (PRIVATE)

"My biggest concern is what all of this has done to me inside."

Face the gradual destruction of her face, the facts: each year, more awkward, increasingly distrustful, tentative, frightened . . . —record each wrong ragged incomplete uncertain gesture; each bout of oppressive, resentful silence shattered by rage or grief; the physical frailty she seemed to flaunt along with the list of her unmet desires, her constant, impossible needs. Inchoate anger, bewildered disappointment. Note that she rushed from the table (*"write it"*), furious, hurt, and probably (the ice—all that was left of her large clear drink—crashed as she slammed the glass down) more than a little drunk. The *unforgivable* (the truth of the words tested by their—on her sobs—breaking almost into noise) passing for the *necessary*. The "truth" she alone could, bravely, at that moment, reveal—some of which might have been useful in another context—mostly warped, perversely mean, or only meant to call attention to herself. *Come back to tell you all I will tell you all.* Her crumpled napkin blossomed at her deserted place. Remember her heavy, fragile, helpless, ugly body, her ravaged face. Looming, suddenly huge, screaming, "Why don't you . . . "; "why *didn't* you . . . ." Don't forget her terrible headaches, we would leave her alone please now at once in a room left dim, draw the curtains shut the door gently don't go anywhere without telling me don't say anything. How she needed our silence. Of course she'd wanted children, *of course* we had been

To my embarrassment, I have sent you a letter meant for someone else.

The Detective story is a kind of intellectual game. It is more—it is a sporting event. And *Water book, book of broken silences, darker shifting shreds and tatters of what wasn't on the shore*

there are very definite laws—unwritten perhaps, but ("if these walls could speak") nonetheless

or the color of the sky, at these angles, reflected back, interrupting what you might recognize

binding, and every self-respecting concocter of literary mysteries lives up to

(lips closed and faintly vibrating voice in redirected flow the preceding position momentarily "'held'")

if only the movement would, for once, just

1.   The reader must have equal opportunity for solving the mystery. All clues must be (choose *one* of the following): A) plainly described in a language universally admired for its transparency; B) nailed like illegible bronze on the futureless future; C) my white wine. You really did fuck up here—so absolutely unconcerned with working with me on the relationship you made me feel like an object to be disposed of instead of a member of a partnership that will dissolve. In a fog so thick they can see nothing of what he imagines must be the beach, but a circle of hard, damp sand the booming of the invisible surf seems to shake. "Alone at last." He's dressed as for any investigation and she—pale as the salty mist which walls off the rest of the world—is wearing a bathing outfit which seems, even to his eyes, just a little too beaded, sequined, and feather-trimmed to ever *really*

2.   No willful tricks or deceptions may be played on the reader other than those played legitimately by the criminal on the detective himself. As well, and most painfully, you didn't give us a chance, since for one thing you were lying like mad. A fantasy formed for the mind's eye only, he suggested, refilling their drinks, a suggestive collection of objects for those who know how to look or rather to *find*: drifted sand in the shape of a woman's belly and hips, if you stand right here, if you

squint, that drying clump of seaweed a little like long hair falling forward where the green glint of polished beach glass seductively winks . . . —the question is how we learn to recognize the semblances, how we come to know when and where we should think "This is like

3.   There must be no love interest. The business in hand is to: A) bring a lovelorn couple to the bar of justice; B) bring a criminal to the hymeneal altar; C) give the reader of the Instructions a certain freedom in the positioning of the clouds in their box of sky. Shall we say that to marry is to say a few words? I have never seen anything like it. To take a knife and cut, right here—she lightly traced a narrow rectangle on his skin—a window, to see right through you, completely transparent, to get some air, or just a little more light on the

4.   The detective himself, or one of the official investigators, should never turn out to be the perpetrator who singeth all night with open eye in the third person while his appeals pend. I will certainly be wary of men with good manners: they appear content and then walk out one afternoon after folding the laundry, citing a failure of desire. But she was perfectly harmless, the last person I'd have said to invite violence. One can't go on saying how shocking it is: words seem to lose their meaning with repetition. The parts were scattered. But I suppose we all feel the same. (Requests the pleasure of your company.) The whole thing is

5.   The culprit must be determined by logical deductions—not by accident or coincidence or unmotivated confession. Does this not strike you as an absolute travesty of human love?

6. The detective novel must have a detective in it; and a detective is not a detective unless he made a calculation, and went for it. I was the loser in that. With one hand she tries to hold the slick edges of the cut together, with the other she scrubs away the footprints she can reach. There was an extra click on the line, something odd about that drink, a dark shape . . . —something I should have remembered, but what? All I know is that no two fingerprints are alike. *Can't you imagine something other than*

7. There simply must be a corpse, and the deader the corpse the better. But what really happens in relationships is that desire and even romantic love *cycle*: people bear with the bad times, hoping there will be A) a sequel; B) a face "in the misty light"; C) a submarine, nuclear and protective like a mother. This was all ocean once. Some of it spilled and she got down on her knees. Where is the "relationship" located? "Here's a shovel," he said, "get busy." Widely gesturing as if to describe description's failure, insistent, the words blurring into meaningless

8. The problem of the crime must be solved by strictly naturalistic means. Such methods for learning the truth as slate-writing, ouija boards, mind reading, spiritualistic séances, crystal gazing, and the like, are as dead as tragedy. If you had spoken to me, I would have listened to you. I would have been scared and worried, but I could have reached you in whatever space you were in. We could have reached each other and found love again. But you lied to me, and you probably lied to yourself as well. Her bruised thighs—seen through the drilled peepholes—flop open. Slightly off center there's her sex: a "hole," a "lack." Another wound the blind blade of the unsatisfied gaze gashed, where it failed to find itself mirrored back as what

9.   There must be but one detective—that is, but one protagonist of deduction—one *deus ex machina*. Lucky for you that the world is a various garden of shallow delights, with the occasional plunge into the depths (but never lingering there) risking these failures of pressure. Close-up of the letter, just as the tide comes in and—rolling back the stone she'd set on the single page—pulls the paper back into the surf, a glimpse of phrases softened to incoherence by their stint in the drink. To "see how they work." The *Coup de ventouse* for instance: the body sucked in shreds up through the air-pipe to

10.   The culprit must turn out to be a person who has played a more or less prominent part in the story—that is, a person with whom the reader is familiar and in whom he takes an interest. Oh, you have done *so* much damage to women, and you have done it out of weakness and arrogance and a concern for yourself that left nothing in its wake. Even at that early date those shifting sea contours were recognized, which make chart revision a never ending task. Lucky for me that there are people who value the enduring. Wave after wave: the overall effect should be as of a hand repeating this gesture across the surface of a blackboard, smearing the lesson until there's nothing but

11.   A servant must not be chosen by the author as the culprit: the culprit must be a decidedly worthwhile person—one that wouldn't ordinarily come under suspicion. And, yes, it is hard to be appraised and found wanting. But just now we wish rather to fix some precise meaning to the term so that

12.   There must be one culprit, no matter how many murders are committed . . . the entire indignation of the reader must be permitted to concentrate on A) a wonderful

polisher of bronze or B) a single black nature. You are leaving me for a fantasy. Weak—and deadly. All of your relationships are ultimately about this ego of yours, your big needs and quests which you can't articulate but nonetheless are the point of your involvements with women. Part of the answer is that for all the advances in science, the sea remains a mysterious—and mystical—force. I remember I was alone in the car. On the radio, the commentator started talking about eight or nine different reports of domestic spousal abuse calls from my house and I had to say to myself: Where in the hell does that number nine come from? I can say it was devastating. Since the 1960s, every achievement in the space program has been covered so minutely by the news media that outer space has a familiar feel. But once you slip below the ocean's waves, you enter a dark, unpredictable and often claustrophobic

13. Secret societies, camorras, mafias, et al., have no place in a detective story. A fascinating and truly beautiful murder is irredeemably spoiled by any such wholesale culpability. BUT YOU DIDN'T INVOLVE ME IN THIS. *A hole, a lack, a grave, a bloody pit, gleaming.* "I will go, eyes open, into my torture." You have the power of the appraiser—the snob with the keen eye, the consumer with good taste, the one who rejects, the dealer in commodities. But let us, for a moment, disregard the character of the hero which rises to the surface and grows visible—and which at bottom is nothing but the light-picture cast on a dark wall. Could this Exhibit 1 have been changed in such a way so as to bring it within the category of your definition of what you regard as a work of art? That is what it boils down to. Only as the letters dissolve and float free of the pages set loose in the water do we get close enough, as readers, to guess at what they might

14. The method of murder, and the means of detecting it, must be A) all ye know of truth; B) completely immersed, soaking; C) any clear thing that blinds us with surprise. Never talk about sparing my feelings. Talk instead about not being willing to be honest; that's your problem. He studied the tide schedule closely. The dagger was an afterthought. I assure you, nothing has been touched. The body sewn back together, edges not quite

15. The truth of the problem must at all times be apparent—provided the reader is shrewd enough to see it. By this I mean that if the reader, after learning the explanation for the crime, should reread the book, he would see that the solution had, in a sense, been staring him in the face—that all the clues really pointed to the culprit—and that, if he had been as clever as the detective, he could have solved the mystery himself. I didn't know this side of you, this core of unfulfilled desire, that's why I wanted to know what you were thinking. In the water a figure of ice: burning as he tries (but she slips from his hands) to lift her out. That the clever reader often does thus solve the problem goes without saying. She appears again, just out of reach, a smooth block of salt or ice or a reflected cloud or a tangled white sail or veil of some sort. She dissolves and vanishes, disintegrates. Gasping, he draws his stinging hands up, empty, from that

16. A detective novel should contain no long descriptive, no subtly worked-out, no "atmospheric"—such matters have no place in a record of. They hold up the action, and introduce issues irrelevant to the main purpose, which is to. There must be sufficient descriptiveness and character delineation to give. Lucky for me that there are people who care about more than putting words together in a poignant way,

who seek a more-than-aesthetic transformation. *That is not what I meant at all, that is not*

17. A professional criminal must never be shouldered with the guilt . . . [a] really fascinating crime is committed by a pillar of a church or a spinster noted for her charities. I guess it boils down to there being two types of men. He explained the smell at first as a problem with his aquarium, and then as a problem with the sewer system. My ex-wife is dead, buried. Once she is buried there's no more story. But if I can appear to be guilty it's a great story, and it starts to make money for

18. A crime in a detective story must never turn out to be A) an accident or a suicide; B) a state of mystical self-abnegation and oneness. I want you to know that if I ever seemed fragile, it wasn't TRUE. You may have been pretending to yourself that you needed to worry about little fragile me, and I may have thought so myself, but once

19. The motives for all crimes in detective novels should be personal . . . . It must reflect the reader's everyday experiences, and give him an outlet for his own repressed

20. I herewith list a few of the devices which no self-respecting. They have been employed too often, and are familiar to all true lovers. To use them is a confession of the author's. (A) Determining the identity of the culprit by comparing the butt of a cigarette left at the scene of the crime with the brand smoked by the woman who writes, I don't want to be a commodity anymore. Hacked into a series of failed explanations because the problem of identification. Not to speak *for* but *with*. (B) The bogus spiritualistic séance to frighten the culprit into giving himself away. I'm

not the one. (C) Forged fingerprints. *And what once moved us like a hollow sigh from the heart of being . . . .* (D) The dummy-figure alibi. He has proof of it in this other woman. She kicks off the green satin heels, lifts her long skirt over one arm, and walks straight out into water so cold it has the effect of isolating each bone in a pain that feels bright. She lets the tide take the gown's heavy sequined fabric, green glitter into glitter, until the ocean closes over her like static in which the melody is finally lost. (E) The bark that doesn't dog us, revealing how familiar these intrusions are. I append a floor plan of the library: "I hired you to find my wife, Mister . . . . " (F) The discovery of a twin, or a relative who looks exactly like the suspected, but innocent, person: lying just underneath the sand, deep enough to be completely invisible, still on her shut lids the pervasive golden light. (G) The hypodermic syringe and the knockout drops. So this is the last thing I have to say. Thanks for all the sentimentality. (H) The commission of the murder in a locked room after the police have actually broken in. Even the shoreline is varied. I don't want to be a commodity anymore: you can be discarded. "Normally," he remarks, "it would be a mistake to disturb the evidence, but . . . . " (I) The word-association test for guilt. So how do you tell if something succeeds? Or if it comes close? What does that mean? Does it mean you feel a certain shiver in your bones? Does it mean you get a wonderful feeling that this is what you have been looking for? That this is the right commodity? What does it mean to you? The object now under consideration is shown to be for purely ornamental purposes, its use being the same as any piece of sculpture of the old masters. It is beautiful and symmetrical in outline, and while some difficulty might be encountered in associating it with a bird, it is nevertheless pleasing to look at and highly ornamental, and as we hold under evidence that it is the original production of a professional (J) The cipher, or coded letter, eventually unraveled by the

JUST THIS

Wave after wave: the overall effect should be as of a hand dragged again and again

across the surface of a blackboard, smearing the lesson slowly past

Her body opened and sewn up badly, sloppily, carelessly, in an awkward mismatched

"Y" so she looks like a puzzle put back together not quite

Undulating blue in blue, a current of departing water furrows the

Her utterly calm expression, eyes shut, as though from some distance

"One fine day I would float to the surface, quite drowned, and supremely happy with

my newfound selfless self. Or I could devote

A whiff of bitter iodine mixed with the stench of

I pressed the raised carving and watched as the bookshelves silently pivoted, revealing

As though writing it down, even as the most simple list, contaminated the evidence

and made the implications harder to grasp. The report's available, of course, but the

words describing these events drift further and further from the

Would the witness care to make

The normal units of reference may be suspended: for instance, if I was to say "Go

and catch . . .

The door was locked

If you go back to the first page you can see

In the hard, dark, wet sand at the surf's edge he etches a heart, scrawls both

The white blanket of fog laid softly down over the beach with that exquisite courtesy

we give sometimes to those who no longer need or expect

Small waves scurry over the footprints, softening the outline in frame after frame but

Wave after wave after wave: the overall effect as of an open hand repeating a senseless

What a grave error to think we could ever have

She raises one hand as if to brush something away or to halt a blow but the gesture is weak and vague and she seems hardly conscious of the effort as though she attempted to ward off something in a dream or she resisted some attempt to

"Readers who do not care for the past should begin at

Famous last words. A diminishing wake frets the private beach. There's a whiff of bitter iodine mixed with the stench of dead fish. The water's a troubled brownish green in close and then a color like pale jade or some unpleasantly strong mint; on the sand, heaped rust-colored kelp; the strewn fragments of white and iridescent blue: broken, empty, shells. Thin, shrill cries of the sandpipers in stuttering run along the edge of the surf; squeals of gulls. "I get your mother's voice and the waves," she sighs, "mixed up: it's the way she'll say something and then take it back, 'Yes,' she'll say, and then, 'no, it's . . . . '"

"And so it went on, the patient questioning, the meticulous taking of notes, the close watch of suspect's eyes and hands for the revealing flicker of fear, the twitch, the tensed reaction to an unwelcome change of

If you go back to the first page you can see that the author gives the whole game away there, placing the clue in plain sight, but—cunningly—long before the reader has any reason to look for it. I see you are an amateur of murder, Mr . . . . He uncomfortably laughed. Despite the scratches on her face and the fact that her dress had been almost completely ripped from her body, she insisted we start on the soup. "Where do these stairs go?" Afraid the other was guilty, each of them tried to confess. "Who else knows about this?" Well, sometimes you just have to say *something*. "I see you are also a student of the darker arts." I raised the carving knife. "Oh darling," he said,

"I know you couldn't have . . . . " Famous last

A knock on the door then nothing

A shadow in the glass just a faint

A fleeting dark shape

But let us, for the moment, disregard the character of the

She stands weeping at the window, "Why won't he

A lingering scent of salt and smoke and

Again the outraged shrieking of the gulls as they heavily

"But the desire to be loved is not itself

A drift of sand in the shape of

"That's his signature alright, but I can't believe he'd

The deserted hallway at dusk

Stained sheets pulled almost

A single blue-green sequin glitters on the trembling hand he

Streaked with torn-up kelp and churned sand, the huge breakers

She must've wanted to be his

Just under the surface, as if

Shell-like ears; pearl-like teeth; eyes the exact green of the

Famous

Which rises to the surface and grows visible—and which at the bottom is nothing but

He pulls the gown from her unresisting body and squirms into it: tugging at the stuck zipper, hands behind his back, sequins falling on the floor like fish scales as he writhes and hops. He yanks the matching teal clutch from her hand, wrenches off the water-stained high heels, unrolls the damp stockings, wraps that double strand of seaweed-entangled pearls around his own neck. He takes her lipstick: leans close to the glass, making a mouth as if to kiss his reflection, while behind him she staggers to her feet, shoving the edges of the wound together, trying to close that hole as though her body were a shabby robe a bit too small, worn late into the day, food-stained, rumpled . . . —she insists she's *fine*, really, pushing at the puckered, bloody edges, holding them in place. She insists it was *an accident*. Clumsily, she scribbles over the oozing aperture with a cheap concealer stick: the flesh-colored grease mixing with

You can't afford to doubt yourself, right and wrong must stand for you as two distinct poles, clearly differentiated: you cannot afford to wander *in that twilight country where the nuances of good and evil cast their perplexing shadows.* You must be kind without being sentimental and meticulous without losing sight of the whole. It's mostly a matter of observation and the laborious checking of

A current of departing water furrows the surface of the bay, darker lines of undulating blue in another blue. The dunes shine gold under the long, low purplish line of the storm front. On the sand, set well out of reach of the waves, there's an open notebook through which the wind, impatient, leafs as if searching out a half-remembered

Worn by the ceaseless movement: to arrive, to depart

Passage

Suspect

He pulls back suddenly and searches her eyes. He says, "I can't tell whether or not I'm supposed to kill you." He rolls away from her and refastens his jeans, stands up. "I'm getting this feeling like I'm supposed to kill you, like you *want* me to." He picks his crumpled shirt up off the floor, "I'm not sure," he says, "but

They serve to further the action

The body opened savagely, as if the murderer had been in a rage to see, to know. To *tear the heart out.* "We have been a little insane about the truth." "'There was a man on the beach holding a single long-stemmed red rose . . . '—that's the story we

Something lived in it once

A cold wind drives the sparkling veil of sand across the beach, rustles sere grasses at the dunes' edge. The sky's almost white, the flashing water a rich blue black like

"Oh, so nobody was here, huh?" A glaucous sequin glitters on the trembling hand he

Infinitely distant. "Where," as Levinas says, "no gesture by the body to diminish the aspiration is possible, where it is not possible to sketch out any known caress or invent any new

Black stones tumbled in a retreating froth of cold white

Same as fast-forwards. I laughed at his threats. Everything we uncovered about her made me more and more unwilling to be even inadvertently the means of punishing those responsible for her death. "Allow me to show you something that will interest you very much." The case was locked. He giggled and sloshed more of the clear liquid into his glass, "A woman like that." A bloody handprint, a muddy footprint: the story told over again from the beginning but with some of the details just slightly . . . . No means of escape. Words last, famous? Dense fog. She lifted her skirt to show him, blushing a bit. "I see you are admiring my collection of native weapons." Despite the agonizing blow he had received, he assured us that everything that could be done would be in order to get to the bottom of this mystery at once. Nothing here has been touched. We observed the procedures. I poured us a couple of stiff ones. You know what doing time means. He'll try again tonight. "This *is* business." But it just doesn't make any sense! Lame as fast words. She sighed and rearranged her garments. If you replace each letter with the one immediately to the left of it—circling back so that Z = A of course—the message is as clear as

If that's what you

I tapped on the walls again, was it my imagination or was there some difference in tone, some hollowness? "I suspect everyone." That door is always locked. When he came back he'd changed somehow, I hardly knew how to speak of it. No means of identification. When you switch each noun with the seventh word away from it in the dictionary the message assumes a less innocent aspect. "I see you know something about torture devices yourself." *Her eyes are open / Ay but their sense is shut.* Despite her gaping wounds she insisted on coming down to tea and indeed she lived long enough to wish each of us luck in the investigation and to describe, at least in part, her assailant. "The desire to conceal by cunning is bedded deep in many people," he noticed. If you're going to book me get it over with. I felt the sharp edge again, yes, this would've done the trick. She stood in the library, trying to explain it. "I see you are an admirer of mental puzzles Mr . . . . " Yes, well. Confusion has made his masterpiece. At this point I like to ask the troubled reader to solve it for

KILLER CONFESSES TO UNSPEAKABLE ACTS

"There is no such thing as being good to your wife"
—Gertrude Stein

THE EXCAVATION

I don't want to speak of her, anymore: I don't even want to admit she existed, once. If I had my way we'd have buried her deep in that gash our researches left in the garden: put her down when we brought up what became, with additions, *The Effigy*. An apology, a substitute, a synonym, a correspondence. Say *There's no such thing* and close the book; tap a muddy shovel on the cover: "the Devonian's long gone now, mate." The actual excavators—as we like to say in the lab—are practically dinosaurs themselves: later it will all be done with light. She liked to watch the way their shovels, shifting periods, shifted the sunburned flesh of their muscled backs. She laughed something down at them from the edge of the dig I couldn't catch. Was it only last summer? I'm writing this in my field notebook, lunching amid the parts I can't make fit. Dust in the sandwich. I'd have liked to know where she was at every second, to have made an educated guess; the switch would've been a relief, to be honest (to contain the claimed effect), instead we closed the hole on an emptiness that can't help haunting, or I, to be honest again (under the hard packed . . .), am inhabited by the thought. What we might have done and didn't. Like the print of itself in fled motion a long-dead thing left: "Despite their name, 'Sea Lilies' are not a plant . . . . " Near the actual stuff it's all experts, I tried to explain, proceeding slowly through increasingly finer recognitions with the tools of an artist or a dentist. From faith to hope to charity, as we joke. Using the calcified, stiff, fragile bones we wrest free of the stone they've become, we cast what can pass for a complete structure, imagining as well as we can what couldn't last. I can explain it all right. Sketched in its "natural habitat" handicapped height on the information plaque, not looking at us: involved completely in the distant past. Monstrous. From the hole I hear them laughing back. And I talk and I talk and I talk.

THE TELL-TALE HEART

1. *the shadow*

I feel teeth chipping away at my sleep.
This is not what I meant
To write. My sleep. My wife.
In the trees outside night comes apart in jagged
Pieces, in pieces which make a strange interpretation
Of trees and night. False dark, false bright.
Green/black. The teeth I use to talk with. Talk talk
Talk. I feel "you" chipping away at "me," at my
Perfect sleep. Hammering. Chiseling. Accusations the blinds make,
Of narrowness: they say you haven't you haven't and by you
They mean me. You haven't. Just what my wife used to.
Something interrupts. It isn't like I wouldn't feel—
Without all this—my inadequacies to the task. I'd feel it. Has the end
Of the deposition been reached yet? The end,
One of the false states/starts. Rattling
Limbs against the glass. For a moment there
I was alone with myself.
I knew what I lacked.

2. *rear window*

My head is a place that hurts.
My moment. Ah vanity, thy name is
My wife. You should talk.
She slumps in the squalor I invented
For her: she is more than loosely based
On The Homeless I pass on my way to work
(I am always on my way to work).
I can feel sleep ticking through the credits.
And I remember this and this and this.
The blinds accuse me of only knowing part

Of the story, of not being willing to_____
(Focus, focus), of making things up.
They remind me I only thought
I hid my sadness. Dismembered body.
Glare of the sulfur lights: sycamore
Boughs in summer seen through a window the shadow
Of sycamore boughs in summer makes
Hush. She's just gone away for a long time,
My current wife, my present,
My second . . . .

3. *the invisible audience*

My wife wants to talk.
This is not my piece of the night, the walls
Murmur. This is not. This is not.
It's the part my wife doesn't want to talk about.
It's not a funny joke.
I send her suitcase away with some of her
Things in it. Plastic bag, tattered
Blanket, cardboard box,
Broken cup. I'm not really sure
What she needs for the trip.
What will she want when she wakes up?
What will she miss?
Imagine a view like the one I've described.
"Like." Now imagine
You have to try see through it.
Luckily there's someone willing to swear
She bought a ticket. One of the candidates.
I can feel sleep. I can feel sleep,
Sometimes I think I can talk
All she wants. But she always seems to be talking
To me but for someone else.

4. *another drink*

My head is a place that
Nobody understands like my wife.
All day the construction outside
Making what I "find" to talk about.
Is there even one true thing,
The floor sighs, you can tell yourself.
Dull gleam. Light (my life) reflects.
The image of the window with its blinds in the dead
TV set. All day the construction outside and
All night my regret. The image of me
Swearing to tell the whole truth:
I don't know where my wife went.
The image of me saying I could say but . . .
(Taking legal advice, taking the Fifth).
The suitcase full of things I imagined she wanted
Rattling like ice in a glass in a trembling hand
Traveling infinitely toward an open mouth. Rattle-
Snake, I imagine her hissing back.
I imagine her: because I can't deal with the facts.
Even that tells me nothing. Halfway.
And again half. Light
From the window about the window
On the cracked mirror, on the table of glass.
Distortions. Perspectives. In *The Alibi*
The door swings shut behind you and that's the last
Of that day, unless they prop it for the guy
With the beer delivery truck. Still you can forget
What it means, for a little while, light: everything
They expected of you, everything you
Expected of yourself. You, you. O, clock. I was trained
In evasive tactics—there's a letter here
Somewhere from someone—about
The best in my class. "One of the *likely*
Candidates."

5. the mystery house

Talk about the moment
When construction stops.
Try to say something real for once, something
True for once. I killed my wife.
I killed my wife. Even that stops, fails
To resonate in the dead space the dust makes.
Talk about the silence
After the silence. Talk about the past.
Talk about the scaffolding, and the net.
What will she see when she wakes up?
I turned my back to the window,
I'd like to say that. I'd like to say
I turned my back to the window and wept.
"And wept": because I can't deal with the facts.
My head is a place with no place
In it. Containing an absence. Nobody
Knows more about that than my wife.
A hole. A witness. I slither my left
Hand across the cover of the closed
Book. Suppose I believed in it.
Talk about a mess. Light making a joke of it, coming in in-
Coherent splintering pieces back. Another false
Statement. The hammer was true for an instant;
The nail made its point. It's not a funny joke.
I sent what it seemed she might have wanted
Ahead of us both, to no address.
I can't stick to my subject. O, wife.
I'm waiting for the words to reach what?
I thought I was building something
But I was only making it more obvious.
My pathetic equipment. My innocence. My broken
Sleep. "She's a one way ticket."
Yeah. And love's a reverse
Doppler effect.

MUCH LESS THIS

I don't want to write about my wife but I have to write
About my wife, I can't help but write about my wife.
Maybe I *am* a "romantic." The way her voice
Disappears when I want to hear it, whenever
She's speaking to somebody else. The way her face
Shuts after I kiss her and the way she thinks
(But there are mirrors and after all I'm not an idiot)
(I can see for myself) I'm not going to look. My wife.
One time on a bridge . . . —but you know all that.
I tell the same stories over and over again,
Making up or remembering details, and
I never finish. The splash and then the water
Smooth again, smooth as glass. The way she says
"Forget it." The long wait for something
A long ways downstream to turn up. And the present
She makes me then of her rage and fear and grief.
Meanwhile long slow stretches of silence,
Or her "rippling" laugh, or the whispery murmur—
I've said this—of her saying something I can't catch
To somebody else. It's not like she's the only one
Who wishes there were some way to totally erase
The past. She's my wife. Still, she's my wife (is, is, is,
Is) (Even now, as I write this) (even now) (I'm not
An idiot): waiting in the waiting room I practice excuse
After excuse; I practice possible reactions—utter
Bewilderment's the most difficult but probably best.
The shoes on the feet of the others gleam as if wet.
"I don't understand." I really *don't* understand:
Sometimes a part of a sentence will reach me
But most of the time the words are so totally
Indistinguishable I'm not even sure it's a language . . . .
But I see my doubt reflected's no longer my doubt.

ONE MORE FOR THE ROAD

1. *I Find a Resemblance*

I don't know what compels me to speak at all,
Much less to talk about my wife. If I had my way
I'd be completely silent, yes "as the grave," even
Like that. At worst I'd make a little sound that was
Utterly private, a sort of quiet *bbbbrrrrr* like a boy
Trundling lightly over the stilled or sleeping body
Of his mother a miniature dump truck, like that:
Bbbrrrrbbrrr, my lips vibrating but my mouth
Shut. I wouldn't babble like this. I wouldn't expect
Comprehension, I wouldn't need an audience.
In a perfect world I wouldn't even have to clear
My throat, much less cough up these chunks
Of self-pitying bitterness: "She won't touch
My cock," stuff like that. (But why won't she
Touch it?!?) It seems "close enough to imagine"
Isn't really that close: in a perfect world
I'd be silent, here I talk. Here I talk dirt. Here
I find myself gagging on clods like, "She doesn't
Understand me," searching—as if for air-brushed
Tits and ass in the glossy crawl of light across
An advertisement's ice—the rocks of the real
Drink: she doesn't. And even though it's by now
No more than a tired joke, it's my life. It's still
My life. She doesn't. She won't. In a perfect
World there wouldn't be all these deflections:
I'd be speaking directly to her if it turned out I *had*
To speak: "Speech opens a door in me," I'd say,
"I feel you shut." Dirt! She doesn't understand
Herself. In the apparently endless memoranda
Made up every day out of what it is or was I'll never
Be able to tell her 'once and for all' that looks like
The worst, but I'm not above those who mistake
A failure of imagination for "innocence"; I'm not

Above anybody a black history's driven west
To the flattest light.

1. *I Make a Resemblance*

My wife has a smile painted on her face.
It's a "willing smile," yes, but if I want something
Done it's always me that's got to manipulate
Her flaccid limbs. If I want it done right. I'm already
Tired of this, and we've only been married,
What? A couple of lifetimes? She says the honey-
Moon isn't over, crying a little, revealing the wistful
Smile I invented, and I see she's lost some teeth.
I don't know why I have to do this; I'm *tired*. At night
She insists we think again about the future, as if
It existed; she insists we look all over again for what
She lost, our fingers tangled stupid in the dust,
In the dark. She makes me tell her everything
I think, I make her make an abstract, her tiny hand
Almost buried in drifts of greasy fluff, ick
(We're under the bed, anyway I can't sleep):
I make her say "ick." I say if she can't get over
The ceremony soon I'll give her something
To really cry about. Oh, the daubed-on tears;
The damp heaps of rouge she calls the "roses"
In her cheeks—when I let her talk; when I make
Her talk, when she talks in my sleep. It's a show
Of teeth. I'm *tired* of this: of disappearing
In the distance in my black, of carrying her in,
Of carrying her out, of speaking the words
She leaves out or "forgets" through the rigid
Smile on my own face, of being eclipsed
Completely by what wouldn't even exist without . . . .
But I'm getting a little ahead of myself. Okay,
White bandages trail from her delicate wrists.
I should have said something before. Stains
Like rust. My wife has only two gestures: *Goodbye*

(A circumspect wave like a queen's: the hand
In the air gently tilting and righting itself) and
Goodbye (a desperate clutch at the emptiness).
I should have said something before but I was
Tired and it's always too late and the words aren't
Ever the right words: tears and a meaningless
Smile and dirty white gauze swaying like Spanish
Moss when I lift her and and hope, she says
She has "hope." In *my* voice. When I began this
I was tired. My wife says she only wishes her teeth
Were as white as her dress, were whiter, were even
More white than . . . . Okay, okay, okay, I say. Stop.

ERRATA

She stinks of gas, my wife, my late
And present wife: the surface
Of the desk is buried in the snow-
Drifts of the drafts of her suicide
Notes; her mouth's full of the rest
Of the bright little pills she fell asleep
Too fast to swallow; the bluish whites
Of her eyes glimmer in the wet slits
Her barely parted lashes leave to us.
The empty water glass. The empty
Bottle of this or vial of that. The bed-
Side lamp left on in the daylight and
The curtains shut. All the possible
Interpretations already in the works.
I see all this because I already saw it
Often in my mind, as did my wife (and
Lived to describe it): her bloodless
Lips; her damp, pale, dirty, frigid body
Adorned with leeches, her bruises—
But maybe I'd better stop. Her bad
Breath thick with the death in her
Throat, the death corrupt within her
She only dug up, from a shallow
Grave, to lie back down with. I saw—
Forsworn and sorry and always too late—
All this ahead of us from the start.

THE WORLD AS WILL AND . . .

When my wife wants to write
About me—when she "has to"
As we say—it's hard. *Immense
Difficulty,* she writes, *each letter,*

*And when I get to the end
Of a word I can't recall what I
Was saying.* Or so I imagine her
Writing. When she "tries" to write.

The absence of memory. The mess
She makes going over and over it.
When she wants to (the dead
Hand dragging across and down

The page); even now she's not
Certain, the blotted apology—
She wonders, she suspects . . . —

Desiring the seismograph's
Thrill: to write in response
To a response to a response?

When she wants to she can't.
Without even wanting to I
Leave her like that again. *About.*

No one hears or sees anything.
The beauty of it. Only a time
Gap, the tainted evidence.

When she finally sits down
To write it all out, at last:
The other side of the story

By herself—hearing someone
Hearing how she sounds
When she's stuck . . . : the fear

Of them rising to offer the right
Word, even the possibility, makes
A ragged hole; she gets up.

Anyway the dishes. Anyway
The kitchen and then the bath-
Room. Anyway the toilet, the

Closets. Anyway the fridge:
The re-frig'er-a'tor. Smells
Like something died in it.

No witnesses to the mess.
She goes back to the blank.

When she wants to to
Which I only add *if.*

If, and the past tense.

IN A DREAM I SPEAK WITH MY WIFE

In the dream I speak to my wife.
For? At? In my dream. In this
Dream. Someone makes the thing
Slow down, has time to worry
About word choice. I think
I cut her throat, though I couldn't
Swear to it. In a dream
I tell her exactly what happened
And she makes me repeat it:
She says we have to get the story
Straight. Our story. When she laughs
A bright bib of blood gleams wet
Down the front of her black dress.
In this dream she says, Okay,
Now where did you find the knife?
My hands are clean, my hands
Are empty; I say if you'd just let me
Write it down, that would help.
I hate it when she laughs.
I speak to her past everything
That divides us, I could swear
To that. When she's past seeing
What she calls The *really funny*
Side of all this she says No,
No notes. She touches a sticky
Red hand to the front of my white
Shirt, and she isn't even
Smiling anymore when she
Says no again. No, she says,
You have to have it by heart.

NOTES

(re: placement)

(And I talk and I . . .)

The whining groan of the earth-moving
Equipment, shifting another load of
The matrix, stamping a pattern of teeth
Marks in the dark stuff description left
Untouched: an as-yet-unnamed period
Where brittle echoes broke in the grasp
And empty shapes shook their dust
All over the disbelievers we were by then—
Embossed on the air—deep in our study
Of the engraved invitations we were
Always about to be left as forever, forever
In that one position, stiff and apologetic
Amid what we'd said but hadn't meant

And meant but hadn't even come close to
Finding the difficult language to set out
In this heavy sea of information to be
Catalogued now with exquisite precision

The flood we poured down to loosen
The stuff she was stuck in, turning
To mud, appeared to amputate the white
Parts lifted above the gooey surface—whatever
We'd got clear, worked over—making her
An archipelago of disconnected fragments,
Truer portrait than any we'd had, or any
We seemed likely to desire *(. . . talk but I get*
No closer . . .) unless our situation receives
Some drastic amendment, and faith
Ebbs, now: painting on marble draperies
The repeated image of an aerial photo-
Graph of a river's mouth, monochrome

Mouth and mouth and mouth and

The delta of speech where it empties
Out against or into the waves' set rhetoric
Brought heavily in from some far off storm
To persuade and hopefully convince

L'AURA

(or, Back To You from *Le Rendezvous*)

I was the only one who really knew her, and I had just begun to write Laura's story when another one of those detectives came to see me. I had him wait . . . .

"'Hello Laura. Comment allez-vous?' dis-je dans mon meilleur style de trileur sobre."
—Alain Robbe-Grillet

lock drop dirt-encrusted cast off   rust semidarkness sketch attempt
blind collar turned up motionless wax   classified ad deaf mute with great difficulty
     any way   in any case show window   step clumsy threatened guilty
     trap steps mess

An idiomatic expression of caution
From now on
She addresses me in the familiar form
She pretends
She addresses me in the distant form

They rape she breaks into she starts
sharp acute right removes
The struggle of the sexes is the motor of history

the street lights mood the way she moves the faces romantic
my professional dedication to decipher a drink obedient careless
old-fashioned street lights dead end street hero of history so called
narrow back street alley pavement steps following pupil of the eye
a rag doll uncertain light knocked unconscious burden landing of the stairs
the door with broken springs with the exception of
fence stage setting fainting spell livid

statue on a tomb showing the dead person lying supine
the doorway gathered unusual strange

my numbness without too much trouble a brass candelabra her slippers
looks me over in a dead faint shrugs her shoulders shaken

the last rites (which may involve touching holy water to the dying person's face)

fainting spells box springs
took them in more or less neglected shelter
wall partition a sprig of consecrated boxwood[6]
can feel a trap

---

6. (broken off and slipped in the frame of pictures of dead family members.)

This poor lighting my own name at the top of her voice

quiver smart streetwise   she leaps wall sconces throws off suspicion crazy delicate
to lie I am anxious to she was watching for
without any caution lights too bright the face the appearance[7]   His ghost
while he was on shore leave a crazy made-up story gypsies circus caravans nightmares
you prowled backstage the lady riders a bit stiff and formal on a honeymoon trip It's
not that great her spouse the sewing machine oilcan hipbone articulations alarm
clock blinking the household accounts the name the Christian Crusaders gave to
their Moslem opponents (lit: a man of the wrong faith) Marie pouts they flirted
(from the old verb *fleureter*) in the middle of changing unexpectedly I pretend I
feign these comings and goings they claimed *to pay the bill* without my knowledge
things become clearer of a tight-fitting shape to my forehead, my temples and my
cheekbones lying unconscious on the ground moreover my free will break the rules
by cheating a crack the stone edge gropingly while enjoying it a linking a succession
chance a treasure hunt   such a suspicious kind of work

temporary to put to the test unnoticed preoccupied me
Don't worry
a half melted sticky piece of candy both tasteless and bitter blindness in hiding unseen
dazed we cross a threshold the best I can I realize the rubbing of fabric scraping
a podium has stopped speaking itching
the eye socket the curve of the eyebrow after all her tone of voice is exactly the same
as if there had not been any (interruption)[8]

nor anywhere else that he must have just plugged back in trick
I no longer have any trouble the (female) lecturer no responsibility falls upon him
He is nothing but a minute link   We are nothing more than slaves a grimace our
carrying-ons

---

7. (This tense, also called *passé simple*, *passé defini*, and *passé littéraire*, is reserved for strictly literary narration, and, as Marie points out, also used in fairy tales and stories that involve an obvious suspension of belief. French children know, automatically, that a story told in that tense is a tale, not a true story.)

8. Although there were only eight Crusades, this is a tale of love and science fiction, and it is logical that a metallic robot should be drafted in an armored regiment! The terms *Moyen-Orient* and *Palestinians* are, of course, amusingly anachronistic, but that is where the Crusaders went, and whom they fought, if by another name . . . .

a bad taste in his mouth as though he'd been drinking too much
that he was not supposed to miss without being able to figure out why
zipper funeral wake glove leather casual who sprang sore out of shape and stained[9]
He had a start casually Before he even went out the door
unless he had gone to get strong (idiomatic use, applied to coffee) some kind of
a worry weariness the dishes the same fast foods signs imitation wood paneling
corner street vendor other miscellaneous cheap goods
His status as a blind man prevented him from being jailed
the size the difference in level out of focus

on the other hand you will miss I follow I venture and speak seemingly pointless
lines while straightening myself up whose convolutions I don't seem to be able to
escape the origin of which I couldn't however define on the crude old-fashioned
paving stones probably not repaired for a hundred years becomes fainter became
double light[10] in contact with the atmosphere seeming to dance for a few moments
on the ground sometimes accompanied night travelers and appears in ghost and
midnight apparition stories There should no longer be anyone living there except
a few bums gauzy ludicrous melodious tones of sirens and fairies in the midst of
which a restless heart a lost soul acute dysfunction with increased intensity the rank
insignia of a chief petty officer I think therefore I am he grabbed her, with both arms
luxuries he stood us up ("I have been stood up" is also said "On m'a posé un lapin")
without losing his nerve without losing his cool his error his boss weird funny
amusing these children a handful supposedly grouchy kids as a last resort a cruising
cab you have missed that are used in kidnappings in the reasonable tone of a grown-
up person threadbare a surgeon's kit a sex pervert while scolding a sight that only
served to increase my astonishment I could have sworn without fear or respect (A
takeoff on a famous motto His coat of arms proclaimed him to be "sans peur et sans
reproche . . . ") to hold onto a succession of tests chance (I felt) my legs giving way

---

9. The Musée Grévin is Paris' house of wax, like Madam Tussaud's is London's.

10. Also called will o' the wisp.

MO

The corpse is angry, hungry. The body's bloated with grief. Impossible, here, to hear oneself think. Unceasing flutter of the notebook's pages, recorded sound of surf, the growl of the motor which lifts and drops the two impasto-caked wooden "waves" which make up this *paysage*, this palpable fake. Alternating voices from the farther room where they're "sweating" the latest suspect. A sighing sound from the lungs when I lift the body to wash it. High in front of the sky-blue scrim, painted plaster gulls wheel by on tethers of fishing line, in the protesting squeak of the rusted, resisting mechanism of the flying carousel. I put the body away. "A million sea birds, / White with despair," he recites. From one angle, he looks a lot like our detective, staring off into reaches the camera won't touch, *off*, blue-gray line of his unshaven jaw lining up with the horizon. There is something he came a great distance to say, if he can remember it. The solution is blinding. Absentmindedly he wipes the prints off the knife and drops it into the surf. The road to Fitful Head, the highway to Ragged Point. Pried up the floorboards and brought the body out again, skin slightly discolored, washed it, dressed it, sat it up in the chair beside me: watching TV and drinking, making comments on the shows. Damp sand fashioned into an ornate moated version of the "slip of a girl" she once was; farther off—behind the heavy wooden door, the broken brick wall—the real thing: older, carrying some weight on her, hair like a nest of stilled snakes. Intent. Malice. Forethought. "That's what poetry is supposed to do," he says he realized, "it's *supposed* to make you cry." "What does it mean to say 'Now I can go on'?" The detective is? *The corpse is . . . ?* Not in the world, but its limit. I cannot unravel the complexities of this case. Impossible half-light; that thick fog blown in off the dry ice dries the throat out; grind of sliding stuff, densely packed adjustments still slipping into place. Places. Face shadowed above the fragile structure, wet sand sliding out of the fist she stays to create

You: no tracks no prints no evidence / I: the cold reproach

Who would notice if we were to completely and *mysteriously*

Say you want to escape justice, hypothetically, of course. A millionaire is sleeping in the last room: all of the doors and windows are locked. Here is an open notebook, pages still blank. In the last room is a detective, who, weeping, kneels to touch those chill lips with his own, murmuring "Please talk to me, please, please, just . . . . " You are charged with abandoning a body, hypothetically, of course. "Tell me what you want," he murmurs. Do you leave by car or by train or? How would you vanish forever? Here is that same notebook, all of the pages erased, coming apart as

The threadbare curtain of drifting fog lifts slowly to reveal a vague expanse of sand dotted with dark clumps of rotting kelp, surf in the distance, shining black rocks in the foreground between which the eye-shapes of tide pools, in one of which unfurls, like the intricate petals of water flowers, blood from a wound held just under the surface. A trick of the light or the lack of it the way the body seems to be dissolving back into sand now, or a body made out of sand seems real for a moment in a trick of the changing light. *Where did my life go*, she seemed to be asking (he notes), some cliché like that: a brittle confusion marred her face. I wanted to understand her, or that's what I told myself, but it was already too late: they were anxious to move her, to carry her off, to shift her down the coast to the next scene. *Crime is money*, they laughed, *Crime waits for no one*: you can't keep her here forever. She was meant to be this mud-smeared broken puppet, our perfect victim, doesn't that face cry out for a few good bruises, shouldn't these big eyes be black? In a torn dress and shredded stockings, a steak pressed to her cheek, she wins the bimbo contest, takes the cracked crown: abandoned, limbs akimbo, beside some stretch of rarely visited asphalt, or any place else. We'll use her again. In dreams she never changes, never rots, is not a desiccated skeleton or a lump of decaying meat. No parasites. She is not. She is never collected, finally—the parts scavenging animals left—in a plastic bag and taken down to the morgue for analysis. There's no failed attempt at identifying the mess. In memory she stays forever exactly as

Hurrying alone out to the parking lot which is the last

A drying tube of "wine-dark" lipstick, one pearl earring, a single dusty silver high-heeled sandal, that long green sequined gown stuffed in the back of your closet, a faded photograph of you laughing on some beach. The way those who'd known you when you were young would speak of your beauty, searching my face. What happened to

"It's not you," she says, "it's your father. I can't believe that—in my condition—*I'm* the one who's going to have to find the knife," she shakes her head disgustedly, "and make sure he wiped

Surely the changes of tides and waves and seasons, the alternating exposure to sun and air, and then to salt water make the shore a difficult

"Talk." Swollen eyes battered almost shut give a bleared glimpse of stained concrete floor, a drain in it. "Talk!" Cracked glass of a window X'd with peeling masking tape, fog sifting in dank and sweet. Those who insist on being able to distinguish the words under the music will find their desires met. But tell me, how would you vanish? The personal always intrudes: the body on the beach becomes the body on the beach on the shining dust jacket of *The Body on the Beach* in the hands of a woman who said you were killing her. Really. Sign this. Dark fish slip between the raised stirrups, hover over the empty exam table; invisible currents stir the abandoned lab. coat, algae darkens the useless keyboard, and dissolves the leather strap of the stopped watch. It's the old problem of the locked room, the closed space. *I have run out of similes, I have run out of words for this complete absence of*

Accordingly he put the prologue before the exposition, and placed it in the mouth

A trick of the light or our looking, this glittery waterfall or sunset: the lush pink 19th-century barroom nude, rupture slightly off-center as if to speak of how and where she might be dismembered, or where a space for memory opens up. "The scene of the crime, the perfectly innocent empty beach . . . ," the Inspector muses. "Men standing around minutely examining nothing, a patch of extremely unremarkable sand at best, the absence at the center, and so forth." In the silence she makes for his speech. Even if he doesn't seem to be paying any attention to the actual, right under his heels, we know he's thinking about it all the time, that in some way—difficult to pinpoint exactly in words—he *is* thought. "A sort of conceptual or performance piece, eh? A murder investigation without a victim, hermeneutics reading itself, forensic science turning its gaze on everything indiscriminately: fingerprints everywhere, endless clues: everything a memorandum, dripping with significance, the investigation going off in all directions at once, bird dog in an aviary, so to speak . . . . " Gaze fixed on the western sky, he goes on talking to himself or addressing the trapped audience in some buried room in his past, shuffling absentmindedly back over the second set of footprints. "Of course it was nothing but botched stabs, fragments, repeated attempts at laying to rest a subject matter, frame after frame interrupted again to be put back together (if at all) in no particular order, for no order can claim a resonant authenticity for itself. What might look like an accident, or a succession of accidents. Yet the tragic idea informing the effort remains the dream of the complete absence of feeling, to be *finished* at

Remember: the doors and windows are locked from the inside. (At this point I always like to ask the reader to

But I don't know what happened to me, she faltered, staring unseeing at the bloodstained sand on which she rested her cheek—I used to be a woman who had a certain sense of style. "I put talc on my face to erase the living colour. I smear charcoal under my eyes to accentuate a hollow dark look. I put pale blue on my lips." The air in the office dank and bitter; the chair she'd sat in drenched, a broken length of seaweed scrawled across its seat; on the floor damp traces of footprints, each one numbered as if to instruct or remind us of how the story goes, what happens next: How the Jr. Inspector is sick once, violently, turning back to what's left of the body a face as white as the handkerchief pressed to his lips; how the medical examiner shakes his head and puts on a mask before kneeling down to his work; how the dead-eyed photographers stumble blindly through the scene, hoisting up at intervals bright flashes of what will have to pass as comprehension; how press crews strain the police tape, a chorus of ragged voices screaming questions and accusations; how crowds of searchers tramp down the long wet grasses and weeds, obscuring the signs they seek; how hard it is here to hear yourself think, the seashell sound of a freeway nearby or the hiss of retreating waves and nothing to go on but what's been scraped up from a shallow grave into a remains pouch and carried off, and the workday dialogue—"Been there a long time, hasn't she." "Too long to get an ID?" "We'll see . . . "—shoring up a realism equally necessary and precarious. He shuts the wall safe, pours out a couple of stiff ones, taps his glass against hers and swallows the burning fluid in one gulp. But his guest—client or suspect—isn't drinking: she's slumped in the opposite chair, slack-jawed as if sleeping, the tagged left hand (with which she might have lifted her glass in answer to his muttered, *Mud in your eye*) stilled, caught in translucent layers of

Set the same with your sailing compass, how it beares off you, drawing also the form of it in your book . . . draw the manner of biting in of every bay, and entrance of every harbor, note the slake or still water . . . and what force the tide hath to

There is a place on the formed body that is "insufficiently formed," and so a place of possibility. The union fails because she speaks. She dies giving birth and he goes to seek her in the land of the dead. She asks him not to look upon her but he does and sees her rotting corpse crawling with maggots. *Sitting here in jail, I feel that I've been denied the right to properly mourn.* At the pass dividing the land of the living and the dead, the two face each other and finally announce

"But that is not what happened, or certainly not all of it. Indeed, if you look carefully," (pointing at the wound) "you can see this was added almost as an afterthought. She was possibly suffocated, possibly drowned; it's very likely that she may have killed herself, we'll know when the tests come back, but put it this way for brevity's sake: a lack of air, of breath . . . , stop trying to read so much into the scene, the evidence, the . . . —ah, so there *was* a note? I'll come back to that—false leads, red herrings dragged over a trail cold as ice, missed opportunities to face, very simply, the facts. Start again with the body: look how she let herself go, yes? She lost her interest in living, long, long before she lost

Bring thence the mappe of that country

She yields to every caress, shudders with pleasure if he so much as looks at her, opens herself to his exploratory hand or hard cock, wears dresses without underwear so as to leave herself constantly available, as he wishes; of course his friends enjoy her. She smiles back at him, serene, while the gang he's invited over takes turns tearing up her ass, she only asks when he'll be back, in case he'd like a hot dinner; she could mix him an i-icy mmm-martini-i-i-, just the w-w-way he

"We are the broken instruments

Both things, both the report and the exclamation, are expressions of perception and of visual experience. But the exclamation is so in a different sense from the report: it is forced from us. It is related to the experience as a cry is to pain. Imagine a land or seascape invented for or by such a cry: unstable location circumlocutions locate, palpable, sensuous, whisper and murmur to shriek to scream . . . recorded as song, "beyond us, yet ourselves"? Those ordered lights offshore were set, historically, by wreckers—whose livelihood was grief. A setting given up and taken back, insecure, scattered and shifting, dispersed, permeated, not central, a sadness, adding salt to salt, empty but for the desire to please, to charm, to succeed, to survive. Need, terror, anguish—and rage, of course. And then an anxiety—laughing ruefully and passing a hand over her brow as if to smooth it—about the way those emotions mark the face. Laughing *musically*. To live with the recognition of one's complete betrayal of one's self: a suspicion growing more relentless in its rising estimate of exactly how much one gave up, for what? For the power to briefly appear—to someone as confused as oneself—as what was *wanted* . . . in order to fulfill the terms of a contract neither one of us had the tools to question, much less

"Do you have a body?"

"Sir?"

The scene is the Chief Inspector's big bright office, on his desk a self-consciously "haphazard" pile of tourist snapshots, watercolor landscapes, books on the sea, postcards ("Greetings from _____ Beach!"); matchbooks and ripped halves of cocktail napkins; endless lists, crumpled and smoothed out and crumpled again, the words crossed out and then written back in and then again crossed out; scraps of bloodstained fabric; glossy 8 x 10s from the crime scene mixed with line-ups of tanned, thong-wearing beauties, buns to the camera, golden cheeks lightly frosted as if with sugar, looking good enough to . . . .

"I don't see a body here." A beautifully manicured hand waved over the mess.

"But we know the women are missing . . . . "

"Church of *la femme*, eh? Ah . . . youth." He lifts a crumpled heap of black lace to his nose for a moment and sighs. "How much time have you spent on this—and still not a single body?"

"Well it's just that, I think that's . . . "—turning the postcard over, he tries to remember why he . . . or if that was even in the file when last he . . . —shrugs, grimaces. There's the sound of a trapped fly at the shut window, buzzzthwonkbzzzzthwonnk. There's the sound of them breathing, a little heavily—and that's all for a moment. "Coffee?" the older man asks, kindly.

Our detective shakes his head, looking down, turning the card, with its faint rust-colored smear, over and over, as if he'd never seen it. He isn't sure he's ever seen it. Another Annunciation scene of course, in this one Mary's a science project: The Visible Woman, the fetus inside her frowning into the tiny hands lifted to cover the face, or maybe peering, nearsighted, into one of those tiny dictionaries, looking for the word for . . . .

"*Habitus* corpus! You can't let your feelings run an investigation! Let me give you some advice . . . . " He closes his eyes. Time, as they say, passes; or rather, a past time rises around us as though a drain had backed up: *a black thick liquid of useless guilt and grief* . . . . He slides the picture back into the pile as his supervisor, almost lightheartedly, continues: "Door's always open! Come back when you've got

Dark sand and bits of broken shell falling from her livid flesh, she stumbles backward down the beach. The wounds close, her clothes dry and mend themselves around her body, in frame after frame it's as though the murderer's hand were zipping up the rent fabric, as though his retreating fist healed the split flesh, taking the blood back. Finally he seems to help her, roughly, back into the white car which reverses through the city to let her back out, unharmed, as if to insist it never, she wasn't. Words last. *Dead not I'm.* The car backs up and reverses away down the deserted street and vanishes. She leans down to the abandoned shoulder bag rising from the curb, spilled contents pouring back into it; a paperback flapping out of the gutter to rest again in her outstretched hand. Already reading she sits back down on the bench at the bus stop, one hand holding the book open, the other at her heart. Rereading until abruptly that uncertain sense of recognition stops: " . . . *sobs and wails and shrieks. So much, sometimes, there's a vague fear—carefully kept vague—they might be hurting*

"I cannot judge or see myself in any of it

Reluctantly, she slips her nail file between the pages—the heroine just heard a suspicious footstep, noticed a dark shape moving through the break in the Oleander hedges down toward the beach, heard an extra click on the line as she said *goodbye* . . . —but it's time to make dinner, he'll be home soon. She gets up, stubbing her cigarette out, brushing ashes off her chest. It's late enough, at last, for a drink. There are two kinds of men: one wants you to be happy forever, one needs your eternal silence, but which

Every answer a desperate

"She kept lifting handfuls of fine sand and letting it pour through her fingers . . . ." *By the sea, by the sea, by the beautiful* . . . . Beside myself. *Same as fast forwards.* Sea sells she shells. Everything held down so long, pushed under (the surface of "Beauty," for instance . . .); let up an instant it comes kicking and spluttering and clawing, "What the . . . ," choked out before being thrust back out of sight. "Nobody must see me weep for victims . . . that is our private grief." Starts: *A shell of her former* . . . . Interrupted questions, coughed-up bits of phrases, gurgling, splashes:

words swallowed once and then spit out, fast and furious in the seconds enough in the air for: "This then is my story . . . . " Partial. *I seem to have merely stood by and watched* . . . . All wet. Blind hands sliding over your face to your throat as if to take you down also: "At this or that twist I feel my slippery self eluding me, gliding into deeper and darker waters than I care to . . . . " Salt water blurred my vision suddenly. See sore. Starts: "I am writing this under observation," or "These fragments . . . . " See, it sells. She shore, sure of

How would you do it? So that no one would know it was you, of course: what disguise would you choose? *Father?* Am I your unbreakable alibi? *Mother?* How did you dispose of the body? Imagine a corridor empty at

Who, if I cried out, among those issuing the restraining orders

"Oh darling," he murmurs. He stoops to take her in his arms, to roll her over, "Don't." He says, "It's a lovely dress," pulling seaweed from the teeth of the zipper; "it's a beautiful dress, it's been a long time, hasn't it? All this unhappiness, no, hush now, you don't have to: I'm here. A sea of tears you fell in, my dearest, don't, you were nearly lost but I saved you, now stop . . . " (he tilts salt water out of a pale green shoe, helps a tiny gray crab clamber from the spangled clutch). "I saved you, I was there just in time . . . . " He unwinds shreds of drift net from her wrists, untangles the looped pearls and kelp around her neck. "I wasn't too late," he whispers, "hush." Later he'll speak of how it seemed to him she was waiting for the courage to bear being conscious, or he'll insist she was hiding out from the uncertainties of life. She seemed lost in a storm of willful expectation, he notes:

constantly disappointed. *It wasn't that she asked anyone else to be unhappy, she only insisted on the inevitability of*

"For me, I admit right away that if I'm going to pay two dollars and fifty cents I want to make sure there's going to be at least *one* murder. I always take a look at the book first to see if there's a chapter headed 'Finding of the Body,' in order to

I hold her up against the dead woman. But which is the model? If I take my hands away, of course she slides off. I pick her back up. From the candle blown out on her entrance a waxy smoke floats slowly up, uncoiling as it vanishes. In the prototype target of murder victims she is not in the center, not exactly what we all think of immediately, not the most like, though it wouldn't take long to see her like that: she has the figure, and her hair—dirty blond—could be right. He carries an armload of lilies; she writes home to her mother: *if I could finish a novel, a book of poems, I would be poreless and radiant.* There is this wound or harbor-like indentation we understand as her sex. Suppose I were to give you a verbal picture: could we say that we understood—in the same way—what we were looking at? If all of the doors were locked? Could we—having argued ourselves (in this conversation meant to restore trust) to silence and glum despair—simply take a walk, wander the shifting edge of . . . ? The wind leafs through an album of photographs of soiled clothes from a grave site. Do they disappear into the light? She reads the parts he's underlined, trying to ignore the marginalia which frighten her a bit. Can I speak of red—if the door is fastened on the inside—without calling it the color of blood? I shut the door again as she requested, left her alone, let her go on reading. *Students were doing a reconstruction based on identical skull castings, yet each sculpture looked a bit like its creator's face!* We seek to install a recognition, communal, "just" (in the vernacular) "the facts": but we have not fully faced the ways our desire necessitates the installation and maintenance of a way of seeing, perhaps. Famous last words. How it begins. And so we come to the victim, the site of an entanglement between various

Was it the door she heard? *There is no such thing as silence.* Turning back to the book she was reading, she saw—as she tried to find the place she'd paused—that the words were not the words she'd remembered, and watched as they blurred into letters and then strange markings, lines, squiggles, which only faintly resembled writing. In fact the book itself was slowly dissolving—flecks of white, traces of . . . —until what she was holding was almost nothing and she got up, her hands open still in front of her, drifting down to the water's edge where the title thins and blurs, even the memory of the words disappearing, her empty hands held out as if she were reading her own palms or another element sliding invisibly over her uplifted hands, a text which changed at every instant, which never ceased moving, held open as if

Thanks to the editors of the following journals, in which portions of this text have appeared: *Bomb, Bombay Gin, The Denver Quarterly, Fence, The Germ, Jubilat, Sliding Uteri,* and *Xantippe.* A Rona Jaffe Foundation Award in 1996 allowed me to find my way into the voice of the Killer, and I am indebted to the kindness of the Roths, A. most of all. "The Evidence" is for D.: "An acknowledged understanding in a moment of silence."